Language in use
UPPER-INTERMEDIATE

Classroom Book

ADRIAN DOFF & CHRISTOPHER JONES

CAMBRIDGE
UNIVERSITY PRESS

PUBLISHED BY THE PRESS SYNDICATE OF THE UNIVERSITY OF CAMBRIDGE
The Pitt Building, Trumpington Street, Cambridge CB2 1RP, United Kingdom

CAMBRIDGE UNIVERSITY PRESS
The Edinburgh Building, Cambridge CB2 2RU, United Kingdom
40 West 20th Street, New York, NY 10011–4211, USA
10 Stamford Road, Oakleigh, Melbourne 3166, Australia

© Cambridge University Press 1997

First published 1997

Printed in the United Kingdom at the University Press, Cambridge

ISBN 0 521 55550 7   Classroom Book
ISBN 0 521 55548 5   Self-study Workbook
ISBN 0 521 55549 3   Self-study Workbook with Answer Key
ISBN 0 521 55547 7   Teacher's Book
ISBN 0 521 55546 9   Class Cassette Set
ISBN 0 521 55545 0   Self-study Cassette

Contents

Guide to units

Classroom Book	Self-study Workbook

1 Present, past and future

Talking about the present; talking about the past; making predictions

Grammar: revision of present, past and future tenses

Writing skills: writing a job application

Grammar exercises
Idioms: *Common idioms with nouns*
Listening: *Gossip*
Common verbs: *do and make*

2 Communicating

Vocabulary: types of written and spoken English; personal communication; learning a language

Reading and listening activity: *The truth about lying*

Vocabulary exercises
Idioms: *Common idioms with prepositions*
Listening: *Varieties of English*
Word building: *Nouns and verbs (1)*

Study pages A | ### Study skills A

Grammar study: *Infinitives*
Language awareness: *Double meanings*
Pronunciation: *Intonation and meaning*

Using reference books
A *Using a dictionary*
B *Finding your way around a book*

3 Making things clear

Defining; correcting wrong statements; emphasising

Grammar: defining relative clauses; cleft sentences with 'It …'; cleft sentences with 'What …'; participle phrases

Writing skills: describing a scene

Grammar exercises
Idioms: *Colours*
Listening: *Radio news*
Common verbs: *get*

4 Sports and games

Vocabulary: dangerous pastimes; how to play sports and games; issues in spectator sports

Reading and listening activity: *Problems, problems …*

Vocabulary exercises
Idioms: *Animals*
Listening: *Cricket*
Word building: *Adjectives and nouns (1)*

Study pages B | ### Study skills B

Grammar study: *Articles*
Language awareness: *Conversational remarks*
Pronunciation: *Where's the stress?*

Dealing with vocabulary
A *Guessing unknown words*
B *Learning new vocabulary*

Classroom Book	Self-study Workbook

5 Set in the past

Talking about past events and actions; reporting; giving extra information

Grammar: Past and Past perfect simple and continuous; reporting verbs; non-defining relative clauses

Writing skills: linking events in a story

Grammar exercises
Idioms: *Numbers*
Listening: *Holiday incident*
Common verbs: *go*

6 Do it yourself

Vocabulary: instructions for common products and appliances; damage and repairing damage; cooking

Reading and listening activity: *They did it themselves*

Vocabulary exercises
Idioms: *Parts of the body (1)*
Listening: *How to do it*
Word building: *Prefixes (1)*

Study pages C

Grammar study: *-ing forms*
Language awareness: *British and US English*
Pronunciation: *Rising and falling tones*

Study skills C

Approaching a reading text
A *Predicting what you will read*
B *Reading for the main idea*
C *Finding specific information*

7 Working it out

Drawing logical conclusions; giving reasons for deductions; interpreting things you see

Grammar: must/might/can't; second and third conditionals; look/seem/appear

Writing skills: giving reasons

Grammar exercises
Idioms: *Parts of the body (2)*
Listening: *Life elsewhere?*
Common verbs: *come*

8 In the market-place

Vocabulary: jobs and what they involve; careers; success and failure in business; advertising

Reading and listening activity: *Dirty money*

Vocabulary exercises
Idioms: *Describing feelings*
Listening: *The new design manager*
Word building: *Nouns and verbs (2)*

Review Units 1–8

Classroom Book	Self-study Workbook

9 Possibilities

Discussing alternative possibilities; saying what things depend on; saying how likely things are

Grammar: will and would; depends (on); indirect questions; probability expressions

Writing skills: weighing up alternatives

Grammar exercises
Idioms: *Streets and roads*
Listening: *Return from Berlin*
Common verbs: *see*

10 Life, the universe and everything

Vocabulary: branches of science; science and the environment; beliefs

Reading and listening activity: *Science fiction*

Vocabulary exercises
Idioms: *Things people say*
Listening: *Reading the tarot*
Word building: *Adjectives and nouns (2)*

Study pages D / Study skills D

Grammar study: *Time*
Language awareness: *Conversational fillers*
Pronunciation: *High key*

Summarising information
A *Taking notes*
B *Writing a summary*

11 Evaluating

Comparing past and present; saying if things are worth doing; talking about advantages and disadvantages

Grammar: time comparison structures; evaluation structures; causative verbs

Writing skills: organising information

Grammar exercises
Idioms: *Other people*
Listening: *Panel discussion*
Common verbs: *take*

12 Yourself and others

Vocabulary: adjectives describing personality; relationships with partners; other relationships

Reading and listening activity: *Skin deep*

Vocabulary exercises
Idioms: *Reactions*
Listening: *Two jokes*
Word building: *Prefixes (2)*

Study pages E / Study skills E

Grammar study: *Pronouns and determiners*
Language awareness: *Regional accents*
Pronunciation: *Low key*

Developing a piece of writing
A *Jotting down ideas*
B *Making a draft and making improvements*

Classroom Book	Self-study Workbook

1 Present, past and future

1 Images

Revision of present tenses

1 Which of these statements do you agree with more?

A Everyone has an 'image', which is the way we present ourselves to other people. So you can tell a lot about people from the way they look.

B You can't tell what people are like from their appearance. In fact, appearances are often deceptive.

Now do this test. Can you tell which of these people wrote the sets of sentences below?

1 I cycle a lot, and I go jogging regularly. These days I'm cooking quite a lot, especially for dinner parties with friends.

I've just come back from a skiing holiday in France – my third one this year!

I've travelled widely in Europe and the USA, but I've never been to the Far East.

I enjoy dancing, especially ballroom dancing, and I've been doing quite a lot of it recently.

I've been playing the flute for quite a few years now, but I still don't play it very well.

2 I don't do any sports, but I like flying kites. At the moment, I'm attending a course on jazz singing.

I speak fluent German, and I've just come back from a trip to Germany.

I love live jazz, and I've been to Chicago on my own a couple of times, just to visit their blues and jazz bars.

I've been eating out a lot with friends recently.

I've been playing the piano since I was eight.

I haven't been to a dentist for about ten years.

2 What different tenses do the two people use? What is each tense used for?

Write a set of similar sentences about yourself, and give it to the teacher. The teacher will read some of them out. Can you tell who wrote them?

2 Past experiences

Revision of past tenses

1 🔲 You will hear someone talking about one of the topics in the bubbles. Which topic do you think he's talking about? Answer these questions:

a Where was he? Who was he with?
b How had he spent the previous day?
c What had happened?
d What had they done?
e What happened in the morning?
f How did he react?
g How did they solve the problem?

What's the biggest surprise you've ever had?

What's the silliest thing you've ever done?

What's the most unusual thing you've ever eaten?

What's the most terrifying experience you've ever had?

What's the luckiest thing that's ever happened to you?

What's the unluckiest thing that's ever happened to you?

2 Work in groups. Choose one of the topics that you find interesting, and tell the others what happened.

Now choose the most interesting experience, and tell the rest of the class about it.

3 They got it wrong

Revision of future tenses

1 The first package tour to the Moon will take place on 15 March 1975.
New York travel agent Jack Garvoy, 1950

2 The last buses will have disappeared from cities by the early 1990s. They will have been replaced by a system of individual computer-operated cabins on rails.
Batelle Institute, Geneva, 1968

3 People will be able to fly through the air in a standing position, using small rotors attached to their backs. This will solve transport problems in cities.
C H Zimmermann, National Advisory Committee of Aeronautics, 1951

4 In 15 to 20 years passenger aircraft will travel at six times the speed of sound (about 6,000 kph) and fly at a height of 30 km. It will be possible to cross the Atlantic in less than an hour.
H Hertel, Technical University of Berlin, 1961

5 We'll be able to provide the Sahara with so much rain that it will become habitable.
Hermann Oberth, physicist, 1960s

6 By 1980 at the latest, thousands of people will be living in giant space stations, thereby solving the problem of overpopulation.
G K O'Neill, physicist, 1955

7 By using radioactive rays, we'll be able to grow cherries as big as apples.
Nuclear biologists, Brookhaven National Laboratory, New York, 1958

8 Trained apes and birds will be used to harvest crops.
Sir George Thompson, psychologist, 1955

9 By the year 2000, the fight against world hunger will have been won, thanks to automation and developments in agricultural technology.
F Baade, Institute of World Economics,

1 None of these nine predictions has come true.

Do you think any of them will ever come true? If so, suggest a date. If not, say why you think it'll never happen.

2 Think about the year 2100. What do you think

– people will be able to do?
– people will be doing?
– people will have done?

Read your predictions out. What do other people think of them?

4 Just the job

1 Look at these sentences from letters of application.
Which advertisements are they replying to?

I have a good sense of rhythm.

I am a trained mechanic.

I am used to going without sleep for long periods.

I have visited Australia several times, so I have a good knowledge of spoken English.

I have three years' experience of working with young children.

I am a qualified nursery teacher.

I have worked as a model for an advertising agency.

I am a good cook.

A **WANTED** Responsible person to look after two children during summer holidays. Luxury villa in Southern Spain. Duties include some light housework.

B **WORK IN** a travel agency this summer. Help required during holiday period. Secretarial and travel experience an advantage.

C **YOUR CHANCE** to be a star. Film extra required for crowd scenes and small speaking parts.

D **JAZZ/SAMBA BAND** looking for singer (male or female) for weekend gigs. Cafés and private parties.

E **PRIVATE TUTOR** required to teach English to 10-year-old boy.

F **BUSINESSWOMAN** seeks personal assistant. Must have secretarial skills. Knowledge of French an advantage.

G **FIFTH MEMBER** wanted to join group travelling overland to West Africa, starting November.

2 Look at these notes for a letter of application. Which of the jobs is it for?

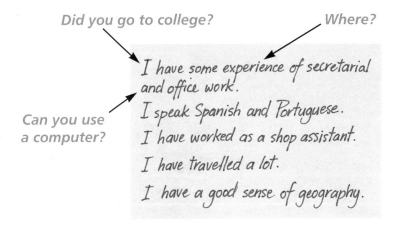

Did you go to college?   Where?

Can you use a computer?

I have some experience of secretarial and office work.
I speak Spanish and Portuguese.
I have worked as a shop assistant.
I have travelled a lot.
I have a good sense of geography.

What else do you think an employer might want to know?
Think of some more questions like the ones above.

Now look at the letter on page 88. Did the writer answer your questions?

3 Choose one of the jobs, and make notes about your qualifications and experience.
Either write real things or make things up. Then exchange notes with your partner.

Look at your partner's notes, and write questions asking for other information.

Using your notes, write a letter of application. Try to include details your
partner has asked for.

Focus on Form

1 Present simple & continuous

Look at these sentences. What are the differences between the Present simple and the Present continuous?

Present simple	*Present continuous*
The sun sets in the west.	The sun's setting.
He works in a bank.	I'm working in a bank.
She often watches TV.	He's always watching TV.
The plane leaves at ten tomorrow morning.	We're leaving at ten tomorrow morning.

2 Recent events & activities

A	He's done the ironing. I've read three books in the last week.
B	He's been doing the ironing. I've been reading a lot recently.

What is the difference between the sentences in A and those in B?

Rewrite these sentences, putting the verbs in brackets into either the Present perfect simple or the Present perfect continuous.

a I'm fed up with living in chaos, so I (try) to get my life a bit more organised.
b I (prepare) for my exams all this week, so I (go) to bed really early.
c I (wash) all the dishes and I (do) the washing. What would you like me to do next?
d – Why are your eyes all red? (You cry)?
  – No. I (peel) onions.

3 Duration

Choose the correct forms of the verbs in italics. Which must be simple? Which must be continuous? And which can be either?

a She's *lived / been living* there for 70 years.
b They've *watched / been watching* TV ever since they came home.
c I've *had / been having* this photo album since my grandfather died.
d He's *had / been having* piano lessons for six months.
e I haven't *eaten / been eating* since breakfast.

Expand these phrases into sentences that are true of you.

a ... for several years.
b ... since I was a child.
c I've been playing ...
d I've had ...
e I haven't been to ...

4 Past events

Look at the sentences in italics. What was happening at the time? What had already happened? What happened next? Write short paragraphs, and add a sentence of your own.

Example:

> *A car stopped and a voice said 'Get in'*
> start running   miss the last bus
> walk home   be frightened

I'd just missed the last bus, and I was walking home when a car stopped and a voice said 'Get in'. I was frightened, and I started running. The car followed me slowly down the street.

a *I heard a noise in the living room*
  open the front door   go to a phone box
  ring the police   close the door quietly
  leave work early
b *I saw a woman sitting on the gate*
  forget to bring a map   ask the way
  stop the car   drive past a field
  take a wrong turning

5 Talking about the future

Imagine that a fortune-teller says these things about your future.

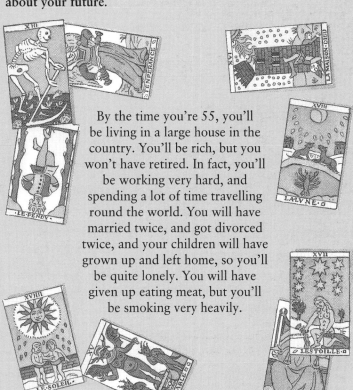

By the time you're 55, you'll be living in a large house in the country. You'll be rich, but you won't have retired. In fact, you'll be working very hard, and spending a lot of time travelling round the world. You will have married twice, and got divorced twice, and your children will have grown up and left home, so you'll be quite lonely. You will have given up eating meat, but you'll be smoking very heavily.

Which of the predictions do you believe? What do you think your life will really be like?

2 Communicating

1 Lines of communication

1 Here are some examples of different kinds of written and spoken English. Which pictures do they go with? How can you tell?

A

It means being open, it means telling it as it is, not opposing everything every other party does for the sake of it. People look to politicians for leadership. And leadership is about having the courage to say no as well as yes.

B

From: cdk@demon.co.uk
To: dave@cityscape.co.uk
Are we playing table tennis tonight? What time?
Philippe

C

Now if we look at the next picture, we can see how fashions gradually changed over the next 20 years. By 1850, women's skirts had become fuller, and waists much narrower.

D

Would the owner of a white Ford Escort registration number P452 JTE please move it, as it is blocking the entrance to the car park.

E

Here's your train fare. Sandwiches in fridge. Have a good time. See you tonight. C.

F

Dangerous Currents
Do not swim when the red flag is flying

G

The Author hereby assigns to the Publisher the full copyright in the Work throughout the world on the understanding that the Publisher shall not at any time assign the said copyright to any other party without the prior written consent of the Author.

H

These days there's so much to read, so much to see, so much to do that our lives are busier than ever before. So where does God fit in to all this? For many people, the answer is, sadly, that He doesn't.

I

Equipment Fair. 9–12 Oct. Berlin. Helen and Mike.
Ken to organise tickets/accommodation, and
check availability of samples.
Meeting with FKR, 10 Oct 12.30.
Helen to submit report by 19th.

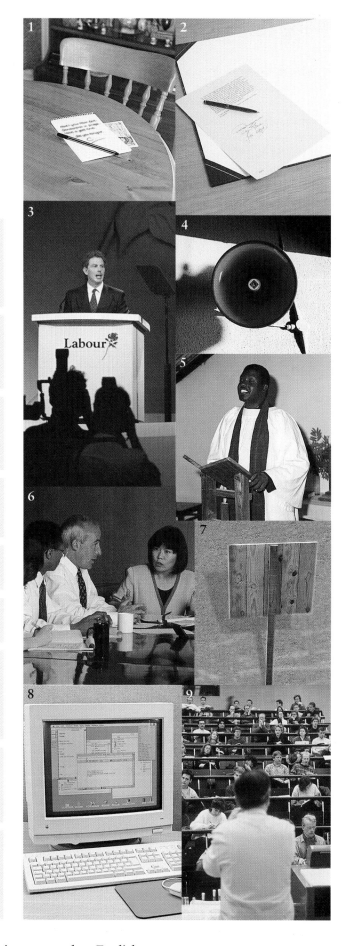

2 Work in pairs. Make up an example of written or spoken English, following instructions your teacher will give you.

Read out your example. Can other students identify what it is?

2 Person to person

1 Match the bubbles on the left with those on the right, to make five complete sentences.

> We used to get on very well …

> We've known each other since childhood …

> … but now we've lost touch.

> … but now we've made it up.

> We've really got nothing to say to each other …

> … and we still keep in touch.

> … but now we aren't on speaking terms.

> I used to write to them regularly …

> We had a terrible argument last week …

> … so we tend to just make small talk most of the time.

2 Work in groups. Think of someone you know (or used to know) that one of the phrases could apply to. Tell the others about it.

3 Learning a language

1 🔊 You will hear four foreign learners speaking English. What countries do you think they come from?

How would you describe their English? What do they seem to be good at? What do they seem to have problems with? Think about these things:

– fluency: how fluently do they express themselves? how well can they make themselves understood?
– pronunciation: vowels, consonants, complete words
– intonation, stress and rhythm
– grammar: how accurate? particular mistakes?
– vocabulary: how wide a range? specialised words?

Think about yourself. What are your own strengths and weaknesses in English?
Make some notes, and show them to your partner.

2 Here are some opinions about learning English. To what extent do you agree with them?

> It doesn't matter how many mistakes you make provided people understand you.

> You haven't learnt English properly unless you sound just like a native speaker.

> If you want to learn English successfully, you have to be familiar with British or American culture.

Choose one of the opinions that interests you.
What arguments can you think of either for or against it?

4 The truth about lying

INTRODUCTION

All these people are lying.
Why are they lying?
What do you think the truth
might be?

A — He couldn't have done it. He was at home with me all evening.

B — Of course I love you, darling.

C — I have never used my position as a minister to increase my personal wealth.

D — Sorry. I haven't got any money on me.

E — Oh that's lovely. It really suits you.

F — If you bite your nails, your fingers will drop off.

G — ALL OUR FOOD IS MADE WITH THE FRESHEST INGREDIENTS

H — We were just drinking coffee and listening to music.

I — I've just remembered. I've got to make a phone call.

Which of the lies do you think is the most serious? Which is the least serious? Why?

READING

The article opposite describes a survey which examined how much people lie and who they lie to.

1 *Before you read*
   Who do you think people tell the most lies to? Put the categories in order (from 1 to 5).

   – mothers   – best friends   – romantic partners
   – strangers   – acquaintances

   Now read the text and check your answer.

2 Choose the best synonyms for the words in italics.
   a their children don't *appreciate* them   obey/value
   b their *offspring* are lying to them   children/friends
   c mums *fare better* than total strangers   have a better result / are more patient
   d and *jot down* whether they lied   describe / make a note of
   e your *hideous* taste in sweaters   terrible/unusual
   f on the dishonesty *spectrum*   list/scale
   g the researchers *grilled* them   selected/questioned
   h mothers can *take heart from* one other finding   feel proud of / be encouraged by

3 Is there anything in the article that you find particularly interesting or surprising?
   Do you think the study's conclusions are generally valid?

Lies, damned lies, and here are the statistics

MOTHERS who feel their children don't appreciate them can add another grievance to the list: half the time, their offspring are lying to them. A study designed to reveal the truth about lying shows that undergraduates lie to their mothers in 46 per cent of their conversations. Still, mums fare better than total strangers, who are told lies an astonishing 77 per cent of the time.

Bella DePaulo and a team of psychologists from the University of Virginia, Charlottesville, asked 77 undergraduates and 70 local townspeople to keep a record of all their conversations for a week, and jot down whether they lied at any time. DePaulo defined lying as 'when you intentionally try to mislead someone', so she would catch the smallest of lies.

The students told an average of two lies a day, while the others lied once a day. They said they had been studying when they had been out with friends. One told his parents that a textbook cost $50 rather than $20 – so that they would send him extra money. Female students constantly told their plain-looking roommates that they were pretty. 'They're everyday lies,' says DePaulo.

DePaulo and her colleagues conclude that people tend to tell fewer lies to those they feel closest to. College students lied to their best friends 28 per cent of the time but lied to acquaintances 48 per cent of the time. In close relationships, people were more likely to tell 'kind-hearted' lies, designed to protect feelings, rather than self-serving lies. 'In short, don't expect even

your closest friend to tell you about your hideous taste in sweaters,' says DePaulo.

Romantic partners fall somewhere between close friends and acquaintances on the dishonesty spectrum. Both students and people outside university lied to romantic partners about a third of the time. DePaulo thinks that unmarried lovers can expect less honesty than best friends because of the insecurity that comes with romance.

DePaulo thinks the results are representative of society as a whole because the two groups had such similar patterns of lying behaviour. She also believes those taking part were telling the truth about lying. The researchers grilled them vigorously to check whether they had written misleading reports.

Mothers can take heart from one other finding. They may have been lied to, but at least their children talked to them. The students recorded telling few lies to their fathers – because they had virtually no interaction with them.

Vincent Kiernan, Washington

LISTENING

1 **You will hear six people talking about times they told a lie. The lies are about:**

- a silver photo frame
- a decorative plate engraved with a horse and carriage
- a school orchestra
- a sample of curtain fabric
- a young child's push-along bike
- a banana.

Try to imagine what lie each person told.

🔊 **Now listen and see if you were right.**

2 **Match the lies you heard with these reasons:**

- to avoid being criticised
- to avoid doing something unpleasant
- in order not to hurt someone's feelings
- to make someone feel good.

How bad do you think the lies are?
Give each one a score from 0 (= completely harmless) to 5 (= extremely serious).

A Study pages

Grammar study: infinitives

1 The infinitive

Can you find the ten infinitives in these sentences? When do we use the infinitive without *to*?

a   When I grow up, I want to be an airline pilot.
b   There were so many good things to eat, I couldn't decide what to have first.
c   You must be careful not to let anyone see you leave.
d   He made me wait for an hour, then he said I could go.

2 Verbs followed by the infinitive

Here are two typical verb patterns with the infinitive:

A They decided to …   B They asked me to …

Look at the verbs in the box. Which of the patterns do they follow?

agree	encourage	pretend	refuse
remind	bother	forget	warn
recommend	remember		

Complete the sentences, using suitable verbs.

a   I strongly .... see the Picasso exhibition.
b   I phoned six times, and finally he .... see me.
c   Why do I always have to .... switch the light off?
d   I don't know why you .... read rubbish like that.
e   I .... go any further without having a rest.
f   Don't .... cleverer than you really are.

Which verbs haven't you used yet? Include one or two in sentences of your own.

3 Seeing and hearing

Look at the sentences in the box. Why do those in A use an infinitive, and those in B use an *-ing* form?

A	I saw them *come* in. I heard them *switch* on the television.
B	I saw some people *coming* towards the house. I could hear them *talking* in whispers.

Read the paragraph below. What did the person see and hear?

As I passed the door, I stopped. A woman was crying. I tiptoed to the door and listened. A man said, 'Give me the keys'. I bent down and looked through the keyhole. A man was kneeling in front of an open safe. Suddenly, the woman pulled a gun from her handbag and pointed it at the man. A shot rang out, and the man fell to the floor.

4 Indirect questions

Notice how we use *to* + infinitive after question words:

– I don't know how to get to the station.
– Can you show me what to do?
– I'm not sure how long to cook it for.

Complete these sentences using an infinitive.

a   Shall I call him Bert? Dad? Mr Smith?
     I'm never quite sure …
b   Should I invite Maria? Fernando? José?
     I can't decide …
c   Shall I read a book? go for a walk? watch TV?
     I don't know …
d   Should I leave the waiter 50p? £1? £2?
     I have no idea …
e   Shall I talk about cars? the weather? politics?
     I don't know …

Do any of these remind you of something that has happened to you recently? Write a similar sentence connected with your own life. Show it to your partner and talk about it.

5 Forms of the infinitive

The infinitive can have various forms: present and past, simple and continuous. There are also two passive forms.

Find all the forms of the verb *tell* in these sentences, and write them in the table.

a   They might be telling lies.
b   I want to be told immediately if anything happens.
c   He seems to have been telling the truth.
d   She should have been told the news.
e   I would have told you, but there wasn't time.
f   You must tell me all about it.

	ACTIVE		PASSIVE
	Simple	*Continuous*	*Simple*
Pres		be telling	
Past			

Fill the gaps with an appropriate form of the verb in brackets.

a   It's their own fault. They shouldn't .... in the middle of the road. (stand)
b   I don't know where they are. They might .... lunch. (have)
c   That jumper needs to .... very carefully. (wash)
d   They seem to .... each other before. (meet)
e   That was a stupid thing to do. You might .... ! (electrocute)

Language awareness: double meanings

1 In English, a lot of words have more than one meaning. What different meanings do you know for the following?

match	light	past
miss	order	present

2 Many other words have the same sound, but a different spelling and meaning: e.g. *horse* (an animal) and *hoarse* (having a rough voice, when you've got a cold).

Look at these words. For each one, write down another word that sounds the same but is spelt differently.

board	weather	been
no	past	through

Now try the crossword. Each answer either has two meanings, or sounds like another word.

3 English speakers make use of double meanings for making puns and jokes.

🔲 You will hear six jokes. What double meaning does each depend on?

Across

1 Kind, sort – write with a keyboard (4)
3 Unit of electricity – sounds like a question word (4)
7 Be on your back – say something untrue (3)
8 Make a sound with your mouth – total, complete (5)
9 Heavy things – sounds like 'stands in a queue' (7)
13 Change – sounds like a table in a church (5)
15 Intelligent animal – copy (3)
16 Was aware – sounds like the opposite of 'old' (4)
17 You make this in a piece of string – sounds negative (4)

Down

1 Story – sounds like what an animal has at the back (4)
2 Bit, part – sounds like the opposite of 'war' (5)
4 Behave – part of a play (3)
5 Revolve – 'Now it's my ....' (4)
6 Central European country – sounds short of food (7)
10 Form of transport – teach someone a skill (5)
11 Leave your car – green area in a town (4)
12 A very small amount of money – sounds like 'posted' (4)
14 You .... a knot – sounds like someone from Bangkok (3)

Pronunciation: intonation and meaning

1 When we say *Mmm*, it can mean different things depending on how we say it. Think of different ways of saying *Mmm*. How does the way you say it change the meaning?

2 🔲 You will hear six short conversations. Listen to the way the people say *Mmm* each time. Which of these meanings do they express?

a Delicious!   *d* Go on – I'm listening
b I agree   *e* I'm changing the subject
c Yes and no   *f* Surprisingly, yes

Listen again, and each time notice what the *Mmm* sounds like. Does it

– *fall* or *rise*?
– start *high*, *low* or in the *middle*?

Try saying it in the same way.

3 Look at these conversations. How do you think the *Mmm* might sound each time? Could it be said in more than one way?

1 A You never did like living in London much, did you?
  B Mmm. I had a very good time there.

2 A I spoke to my father about it.
  B Mmm.
  A And he thought about it for a bit.
  B Mmm.
  A And he said he thought I should take the job.
  B Mmm.

3 A You know Jane quite well, don't you?
  B Mmm. Why do you ask?

4 A Is the soup all right?
  B Mmm. Wonderful.

5 A What does 'mutton' mean?
  B It's meat that comes from a sheep. OK?
  A Thank you.
  B Mmm. Now let's look at Question 3.

6 A Do you like José?
  B Mmm. He's all right.

🔲 Now listen to the recording. Did the speakers say *Mmm* in the way you expected?

Making things clear

1 Definitions

Defining relative clauses

1 Do this quiz, and then check your answers. How many did you get right?

Watch your words

Here are eight simple sentences. But can you guess what the words in italics mean?

1 'Oh Charles,' she sobbed. 'They say you're an *embezzler*.'
  a someone who snores
  b a man who has more than one wife
  c someone who steals money from the company they work for

2 'Don't touch that *toadstool*,' he warned.
  a a frog whose bite is poisonous
  b a sharp-edged tool that is used for cutting stone
  c a mushroom that you can't eat

3 'I spent three years in that *orphanage*,' he said, 'and I hated every moment.'
  a accommodation for people whose houses have been destroyed in war
  b a home for children whose parents have died
  c a prison for young people who have committed serious crimes

4 'I've had enough of this *drudgery*!' she screamed.
  a work that is difficult and boring to do
  b food that has a very plain taste
  c conversations that are really about nothing

5 'Over the years,' he said, 'that *couch* has had some very strange people on it.'
  a a bed you lie on while visiting a psychiatrist
  b a table you lie on while having an operation
  c a chair you sit on while having dental treatment

6 'Nobody seems to use *thimbles* these days,' she said.
  a stone bottles you fill with hot water and place in your bed
  b metal cups you wear on your finger while sewing
  c scissors you use to trim the hairs in your nose

7 We spent the afternoon playing *tag*.
  a a children's game in which one player has to try to touch the others
  b a card game in which players try to be first to get rid of all their cards
  c a party game in which players pin cards on each other's backs

8 'Don't go there in August,' she advised. 'There are *midges* everywhere!'
  a young boys who pick people's pockets and snatch handbags
  b badly behaved tourists who spoil other people's holidays
  c small flying insects that bite

Add relative pronouns to these definitions where necessary. Use the quiz answers to help you.

  a A bouncer is a person .... throws troublemakers out of nightclubs.
  b Slush is snow .... has started to melt.
  c A colleague is someone .... you work with.
  d Slippers are soft shoes .... you wear indoors.
  e A widow is a woman .... husband has died.
  f A crèche is a place .... parents can leave small children while they are at work.

2 Work in groups of three. The teacher will give you a word and its true definition. In your group, make up two other definitions.

Read out your three definitions. Can the rest of the class guess which is correct?

2 Getting your facts right

Cleft sentences with 'It'

It wasn't …   Paul McCartney married Yoko Ono in 1968.   *It was …*

1 The sentence above isn't true.
Correct it, beginning with the words
in the bubbles.

There's one factual error in each of these
sentences. Correct it in the same way.

> Italy won the 1994 football World Cup,
> which was played in America.

> When Little Red Riding Hood went into the cottage,
> she saw her grandmother sitting in the bed.

> Buddhism originated in China in the
> 6th century BC.

2 Write a similar sentence with one factual
error. Show it to other students, and see
whether they can correct it.

3 Emphasising the point

Cleft sentences with 'What'

1 🔲 **Listen to the recording.**
How do the speakers express these ideas?

> I enjoy reading the
> Sunday papers in bed.

> I find phrasal verbs
> really difficult.

> In New York the shops
> stay open all night. That
> really surprised me.

> He never answered
> my letters – that
> really annoyed me.

2 Write two or three true sentences using the table.

What	I enjoy I admire I can't stand I find difficult	about …	is …
The thing (that)	surprises me annoys me fascinates me		

Show your sentences to other students, and
answer any questions they may have.

4 In the frame

1 Here are some descriptions of famous works of art.
Do you recognise any of them?
How could you join the sentences together to make better descriptions of them?

  a This picture shows two men. They are sitting by a river. They are wearing formal evening dress. Between them is a woman. She is wearing nothing at all. There is a picnic. It is spread on the grass beside them.

  b This is a self-portrait. It shows the artist. His ear is missing. His face is wrapped in a bandage.

  c This is a fresco. It portrays God. His arm is stretched out. He is creating Adam.

  d This is a sculpture of a man. He is sitting. His forehead is supported by his fist. He is lost in thought.

2 Here is a brief description of Edvard Munch's painting *The Sick Child*.
How many of the ideas on the right could you incorporate into the three sentences?

The picture shows a child.
On the bedside table there is a bottle.
Beside her is a woman.

She has bright red hair.

She's probably the child's mother.

She's holding the girl's hand.

It probably contains the girl's medicine.

She has a very pale face.

Her head is bowed in grief.

She's leaning against a large pillow.

Her head is turned towards the window.

She has grey hair.

3 Look at your own picture in the back of the book and write a description of it. Include enough details so that someone else could visualise the picture.

Read your partner's description, and try to visualise the picture.

Now look at the picture. How good was your partner's description?

Focus on Form

1 Relative clauses

Student A: **Read out a sentence beginning from Box A.**
Student B: **Complete the sentence with a suitable continuation from Box B, making any necessary changes.**

Example:

A Where did you get that coat …
B … (that) I saw you wearing last night?

Box A

1 Where did you get that coat …
2 I've forgotten the name of that town …
3 Did you hear the joke about the man …
4 I'm afraid this is a decision …
5 There are some things …
6 I really enjoyed that day …
7 What was the name of the Greek hero …

Box B

a You can't put it off any longer.
b We went to the beach.
c I saw you wearing it last night.
d He killed the Minotaur.
e They really make me angry.
f His wife bought him a Porsche.
g They hold the music festival there.

---

2 Embedded relative clauses

Expand these sentences from news stories by inserting relative clauses.

Example:

An elephant has been destroyed.

– An elephant *that escaped from London Zoo and crushed six cars* has been destroyed.
– An elephant *whose teeth had worn away so badly that it could not eat* has been destroyed.
– An elephant *that was injured when it was hit by a train* has been destroyed.

a A man died in hospital last night.
b A woman has been awarded $500,000.
c The house has been destroyed by fire.
d From today, owners of vehicles can be fined up to £1,000.
e And finally, a cat was recovering at home after a six-hour rescue operation.

3 Cleft sentences with 'It'

Christopher Columbus　　　*Marco Polo*

Student A: **Look at the text about Christopher Columbus on page 89. Can you choose the correct version of the story? Check your answers with B.**

Student B: **Look at the text about Christopher Columbus on page 90, and check A's answers.**

Example:

Christopher Columbus was born in *Spain/Portugal/Italy* in 1451.

A I think it was Spain where Christopher Columbus was born.
B No, it wasn't Spain.
A OK. Was it …?

Now do the same with the text about Marco Polo. It's B's turn to choose the correct version.

4 Emphatic cleft sentences

Make these sentences more emphatic by using *What …* or *The thing …*

Example:

This room's got big windows, and I like that.

What I like about this room is that it's got big windows.

a I was always short of money at university, and I didn't like that.
b You need a good night's sleep.
c I enjoy a cold shower in the morning.
d Her knowledge of African history impressed everybody.
e He always tells the truth, and I admire that about him.
f Ants always seem to know exactly where they're going – that fascinates me.
g You don't seem to realise that I work an 18-hour day.

---

4 Sports and games

1 Dangerous pastimes

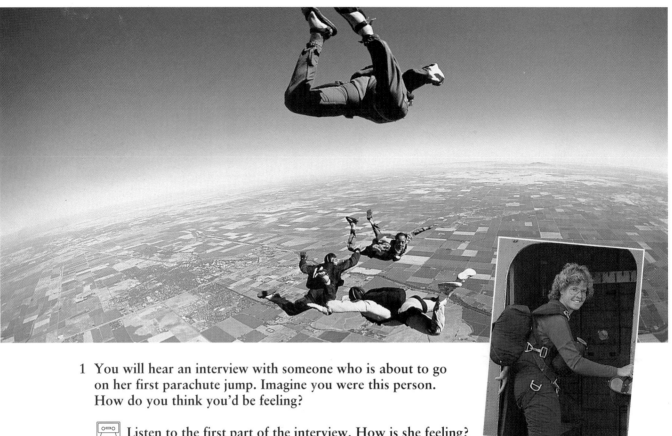

1 You will hear an interview with someone who is about to go on her first parachute jump. Imagine you were this person. How do you think you'd be feeling?

   [cassette icon] Listen to the first part of the interview. How is she feeling? Does she seem to be prepared?

   [cassette icon] Now listen to what she says after the jump. How does she feel about the experience? After hearing what she says, would you be prepared to try it yourself?

2 Divide these activities into three lists:
   – things you'd like to do (or have done)
   – things you'd be willing to try
   – things you'd never do.

   Add one other activity to each list.

   Compare lists with other students. Why did you answer as you did?

A Bungee jumping B Rock climbing
C White water canoeing D Potholing E Off-piste skiing F Scuba diving

2 Play the game

1 Here are some instructions relating to five different games.
What are the games? Fill the gaps with words from the box.

A
When you .... , the ball has to ....
twice, once on each side of the ....
... If your shot misses the table, it's .... ,
and you lose the ....

B
You can only .... diagonally, one
square at a time. You .... an
opponent's .... by jumping over it.

C
You throw the .... , and if you get a 3, for
example, you .... three squares around the
.... If you .... on a property owned
by another player, you have to pay rent.

board	net	score
bounce	out	serve
deal	pass	shuffle
dice	piece	suit
land	pitch	tackle
move	point	take

D
You can kick the ball forwards, but you can only
.... it backwards.
... The best way to .... a player who is
running with the ball is to grab him round the legs.
... If you can touch the ball down at the far end of
the .... , you .... five .... This is
called a try.

E
You .... the
cards, and ....
out 13 cards to each
player. Then the
players sort out their
cards into the four
different ....s.

2 Choose another sport or game and write a few sentences about how to play it.
Read out your sentences, and see if other people can guess what sport or game it is.

3 And now the sports news ...

1 Look at these newspaper headlines.
What would you expect to read in
the stories that accompany them?

**World champion swimmer
suspended after drugs test**

**FOOTBALLER FACES SUSPENSION
AFTER ATTACK ON SPECTATOR**

'Own-goal' defender shot
dead outside restaurant

**Tennis stars strike it rich
on and off the court**

Now read the stories on page 91.

2 Work in groups. Choose any of these questions that interest you, and try to reach
agreement about them.

a Are we right to ban performance-enhancing drugs, or should they be made legal?
b Why is it that there is so much violent behaviour at football matches?
c Do top sportsmen and sportswomen earn too much money?
d 'Sports personalities have a special responsibility to behave well because they
have a tremendous influence over young people.' Do you agree?
e How do you feel when your national team wins or loses? Is it just a game, or is it
more than that?

Now report your conclusions to the rest of the class.

4 Problems, problems ...

INTRODUCTION

1 Read Problem 1. If you can work out the answer, write it down.

Problem 1 In the post

Angela runs an antique shop. Last week she wanted to post a sword to a customer, so she wrapped it up and took it to the post office. Unfortunately, the sword was 100 cm long and the maximum length allowed for parcels is 95 cm, so the post office refused to accept it.

Not being one to give up easily, Angela repackaged the sword and took it back to the post office, who accepted it without argument.

How did she manage it?

2 🔲 You will hear two clues. After each clue, you will have another chance to work out the answer (or change your previous answer).

3 🔲 Now listen to the solution. Did you get the right answer? At what stage did you get it?

READING

Working with a partner, read Problems 2–8 and try to solve them together. If you are stuck, there is a clue for each Problem on page 92.

LISTENING

🔲 Listen to the answers. Score two points for each answer you got right without looking at a clue, and one point for each answer you got after looking at a clue. What is your total score?

Problem 2 Two boyfriends

Annie's flat is near an underground train station. She has two boyfriends, Bill and Mario, who live on the same train line, but in opposite directions. Every ten minutes, a train leaves in each direction.

Since she likes each of them equally, she lets the train decide which one of them she will visit. She turns up at the station, and catches whichever train comes first.

She is surprised to find that nine times out of ten she ends up visiting Mario. Can you explain?

Problem 3 An explosive mixture

The Professor has a problem. He has eight chemical bottles numbered 1 to 8, and they must be placed in a rack like that below. However, in order to avoid an explosion, bottles with consecutive numbers must not be placed next to one another diagonally, vertically or horizontally.

So if he puts bottle number 5 in space C, then neither bottle 4 nor bottle 6 can be placed in spaces A, D or G. What is your advice?

4 Sweet revenge

Sick of the silly behaviour of his pupils, the maths teacher set them a brainteaser:

'If six sweet jars are arranged in a row, the first three full of sweets and the next three empty, what is the minimum number of jars that need to be moved so that they alternate full, empty, full, empty, full, empty?'

Since nobody got it right, he ate all the sweets himself. What do you think is the answer?

5 One man and his dog

Farmer Bob, with his dog, Fang, is walking home at 5 kph. When he is 20 kilometres from home he lets Fang off its lead and the dog runs all the way home at 15 kph. As soon as it gets there it turns round and runs back to Bob, and keeps running back and forward at 15 kph until Bob gets home.

How far does Fang run?

6 On balance

Smuggler Sam Crook has received nine 2 kg boxes of chocolates, in one of which is hidden 100 g of diamonds, giving the box a total weight of 2.1 kg. He wants to open that box as quickly as possible, and fortunately he has a balance handy.

What is the minimum number of weighings required for him to find the box containing the diamonds?

7 Whodunnit?

Three people are suspects in a robbery case. They each make a statement to try and clear themselves:

I was miles from the house.

No he wasn't!

I'm innocent.

A   B   C

An informer has told the Chief Inspector that two of the suspects always lie, and one always tells the truth, though he didn't say which.

Which of the suspects is guilty?

8 Wrong labels

The local greengrocer has just received three large sacks of potatoes. One contains white potatoes, one contains red potatoes and one contains a mixture of red and white.

WHITE   MIXED   RED

Unfortunately, the suppliers have just rung to say that they have put all three labels on the wrong sacks.

Can the greengrocer, by taking one potato from one sack and not looking inside, work out which label should be on each sack?

Study pages

Grammar study: articles

1 The definite article

Look at the examples. Why is *the* used in B, but not in A?

A	*Money* makes the world go round. They sell second-hand *books*. Do you like *men* with beards?
B	Hand over *the money*! I've finished all *the books* you lent me. Do you recognise *the men* in this photo?

Make sentences using these expressions, with and without *the*.

a flowers
b silver knives and forks
c water

2 Article or not?

Here are six rules about the definite article, and one example of each rule. Match the rules with the examples.

1 We use *no article* before a noun followed by a number.
2 We use *no article* for talking 'in general'.
3 We often use *the + adjective* for talking about groups of people.
4 Names of countries, continents, cities and mountains usually have *no article*, but if they're plural we use *the*.
5 Names of rivers, seas and oceans have *the*.
6 Names of public buildings, hotels, cinemas, theatres and restaurants usually have *the*.

a The Nile flows into the Mediterranean.
b I'm staying in Room 420.
c More should be done to help the unemployed.
d Meet me outside the Sheraton.
e I love Albanian folk music.
f The Philippines are in East Asia.

Give one or two examples of your own for each rule.

3 School vs the school

Look at the examples. When do we say *hospital* and when do we say *the hospital*?

A	We live opposite the hospital. I went to the hospital to visit my sister. He works at the hospital as a porter.
B	She's been in hospital for six months now. I had to go into hospital for several days. When's he coming out of hospital?

In the sentences below, the words in italics are used in the same way as *hospital*. Add *the* where necessary.

a He was sent to .... *prison* for five years.
b A lot of tourists go to .... *church* to see the icons.
c I stayed in .... *bed* till eleven.
d She comes out of .... *school* at 3.30.
e I went to .... *college* to speak to the principal.
f She studied physics .... *university*.

4 Count and non-count nouns

Which of the words in italics are count and which are non-count? Fill the gaps with *a(n)* or *some*.

a Can I offer you .... *advice*?
.... *suggestion*?

b I've just heard .... interesting *news*.
.... interesting *announcement*.
.... interesting *information*.

c There's going to be .... *thunderstorm*.
.... bad *weather*.

d She's carrying .... *luggage*.
.... *suitcase*.

e We'll need .... *accommodation* for the night.
.... *room*

f He's got .... strange *equipment* in his
.... strange *machine* laboratory.

g Do you mind if I put on .... *music*?
.... *tape*?

Which of the non-count words can also be used with *a piece of* …?

5 Phrases with non-count nouns

We cannot say *a bread*, but we can say *a loaf of bread*.
What other phrases can you make using words from the two boxes?

bag	jar	sheet
bar	loaf	slice
bottle	lump	tube
carton	piece	

bread	milk
chocolate	paper
flour	sugar
honey	toothpaste

Replace the words in italics with similar phrases.

a I think there's *some glue* in the cupboard.
b Could you bring *some charcoal* for the barbecue tonight?
c Would you like *some more toast*?
d We need to buy *some soap* and *some orange juice*.

Language awareness: conversational remarks

1 🔲 **You will hear a number of short remarks. Listen and match them with the situations they go best with.**

   a You're having a drink with someone.
   b You're checking if someone understands.
   c You're saying goodbye to someone.
   d You don't believe what someone says.
   e A child's hurt himself.
   f You want to start a new subject.

2 **Here are some other short conversational remarks. Do you know what they mean? If not, can you guess?**

   Oh dear!
      It's just not on.
           Get on with it!

   So what?
      It's up to you.
           What's up?

   No idea.
      Whoops!
           Phew!

🔲 **Now listen and check your answers.**

3 **Instead of *Oh dear*, we could also say**

   – What a pity!
   – I'm sorry to hear that.
   – What a shame!

Look at some of the other remarks. Can you think of other ways to say them?

Pronunciation: where's the stress?

1 🔲 **Look at these sentences and listen to what B says. Which of the underlined words are stressed?**

   1 A You might as well take two.
      B But I only want one.

   2 A Do you need an umbrella?
      B No, I've got one.

   3 A Where does Beth live?
      B Well, in fact she lives here.

   4 A Where are the nearest shops?
      B About five minutes from here.

   5 A Who got the job?
      B Surprisingly, they chose me.

   6 A Hello, Bill.
      B Hello. Thanks for coming to see me.

   7 A Where's Jane?
      B She's over there.

   8 A Do you like the new concert hall?
      B I've never been there.

The last word in B's replies is sometimes stressed and sometimes not. Why do you think this is?

🔲 **Listen to the replies again and try saying them in the same way.**

2 **Look at these conversations. Which of the underlined words do you think will be stressed most?**

   1 A I asked John to help.
      B Why didn't you ask me?

   2 A How old do you think he is?
      B Why don't you ask him?

   3 A I really liked that film.
      B Did you? I didn't.

   4 A Did you call me?
      B Yes. Could you come here a moment?

   5 A Do you like cats?
      B No, I certainly don't!

🔲 **Now listen and see if you were right.**

3 **Look at these remarks. Try saying them with the stress on different words. How does it change the meaning?**

   a It's time to go now.
   b How do you know that?
   c They always invite him.
   d I think they've got one.

5 Set in the past

1 Whatever happened to Lord Lucan?

FOR SOME REASON, Lord Lucan was known to his friends as 'Lucky' Lucan. In the early 1970s, however, his luck was beginning to run out, and in 1974, at the age of 39, he found himself in serious financial difficulties. He had lost more than £250,000 at gambling tables around the world, and had been forced to sell the family silver to pay off some of his debts. He was also separated from his wife, and was fighting her in the courts for the custody of their three children.

Lord Lucan in 1974 ...

But worse was to come. On 7 November 1974, Lady Lucan ran into a pub near her home in Belgravia, London. She was covered in blood and was screaming 'He's murdered my nanny!'

Apparently Lucan had gone to the house armed with a hammer, intending to murder his wife. He had been hiding in the kitchen when the children's nanny had walked in, and he had killed her by mistake. He had then panicked and run out of the house, attacking his wife on the way. A police search began.

But Lucan has never been found. On the day of the murder, he sent a note to an old school-friend saying that he was going to disappear for a time, and a car he had borrowed was found abandoned at the port of Newhaven, where police believed he had boarded a ferry for France.

Since then, Scotland Yard has followed up around 60 'sightings' a year in places as far apart as San Francisco, Brisbane, Madagascar, Botswana, Hong Kong and, more recently, South Africa. But they have led nowhere.

... and as he might look now

As recently as 1995, a woman claimed that she had been baby-sitting at the house of one of Lucan's friends on the day after the car was found (she was 16 at the time), and that Lucan had turned up at the door.

So what happened? Did he kill himself, perhaps by jumping off a cross-Channel ferry? His wife thinks so: he was a noble man, she says, and would behave in a noble way. Others point out that you need around 150 kilos of concrete to keep a body at the bottom of the sea – so if Lucan jumped into the sea, why has his body never been found?

Or did he leave the car at Newhaven and return to London (as the babysitter's evidence suggests)? Or is he living somewhere near you? If you happen to see him, Scotland Yard would like to hear from you.

---

1 Read the newspaper story.

   a Here are some events in the order they appear in the story. What order did they actually happen in? Number them from 1 to 8.

     Lady Lucan ran into a pub screaming.
     Lord Lucan went to the house.
     He was hiding in the kitchen when the nanny came in.
     He killed the nanny.
     He attacked his wife.
     The police started a search for him.
     A car was found at Newhaven.
     Perhaps he boarded a ferry for France.

     Which of the events are *flashbacks* (i.e. jump back to an earlier point of time)? What tenses are used for these parts of the story?

     Find other examples of flashbacks in the story.

   b Most of the story is set in the past, but some parts are about

     – the present
     – the period 'up to now'.

     Which are they?

2 Imagine that you sighted Lord Lucan recently. Decide

     – where it happened
     – what you were doing
     – what he was doing
     – what happened next.

Complete this newspaper report about the sighting.

LORD LUCAN SIGHTED?

According to information received by Scotland Yard, Lord Lucan was sighted last Saturday in

2 Difficult situations

Reporting verbs

1 Here are sentences from three separate stories.
   What do you think the stories are about?

> They kept accusing me of bringing in almost five pounds of cocaine.

> A huge bloke emerged from behind the door with a crowbar and threatened to smash my windscreen unless I backed off.

> The girl I had the argument with finally admitted to me that she had scratched my name in the table.

Now listen to the stories. How similar are they to what you thought?

2 *a* Look at the verbs in the box. Which are followed by *that*, which by *to*, and which by *-ing*?

   b Think of something real that happened to you, and write a sentence about it using one of the verbs.

   Tell your partner what happened. Include your sentence in what you say.

accuse	offer	remind
admit	promise	threaten
deny	refuse	warn

3 Background information

Non-defining relative clauses

1 Here is an extract from a story.
   How do you think the sentences in the box fit into it?

There were three patients in the waiting room that evening.
One was Mrs Mancini …
Next to her was young Mickey Wilson …
And then there was my old friend Joseph …
… I pressed the buzzer, and wondered which of them would come in first.

Incorporate the extra information into the story, using relative clauses where appropriate.

2 Here is a later part of the story.
   Continue it with a relative clause of your own.

At two minutes to six, I was just getting ready to lock up the surgery when another patient walked in. It was Hannah Roberts …

> He kept wiping it with a handkerchief.
>
> His landlord was threatening to evict him from his flat.
>
> It wasn't enough to pay all his bills.
>
> She suffered from insomnia.
>
> It brought in a reasonable amount of money.
>
> He had a job.
>
> I had treated him for a knife wound six months before.
>
> She had left him with three children to bring up single-handed.
>
> He'd been living there since he had got married.
>
> She came every Thursday to get her week's supply of sleeping pills.
>
> This time he had a nasty cut on the eye.
>
> His wife had died two years before.

4 One thing after another

1 Here are five similar sentences.
How do the underlined expressions affect the meaning?
Which ones have the same meaning?

A At first, everything seemed fine, but <u>when</u> we were in the air things started to go seriously wrong with the aircraft.

B At first, everything seemed fine, but <u>as soon as</u> we were in the air things started to go seriously wrong with the aircraft.

C At first, everything seemed fine, but <u>the moment</u> we were in the air things started to go seriously wrong with the aircraft.

D At first, everything seemed fine, and <u>it wasn't until</u> we were in the air <u>that</u> things started to go seriously wrong with the aircraft.

E At first, everything seemed fine, and <u>it was only when</u> we were in the air <u>that</u> things started to go seriously wrong with the aircraft.

2 How could you join these ideas together, using the underlined expressions above?

   a got married – a year – discovered he had another wife
   b arrived home – opened the kitchen door – saw there had been a burglary
   c met at a party – started talking – knew we'd be lifelong friends
   d went to teacher training college – started teaching – realised that it wasn't the right job for me
   e absorbed in a book – turned round – realised there was a stranger in the room

3 Work in groups. Write the beginning of a story. Include one of the captions below, and one of the sequence expressions you have practised. Pass your paragraph to another group to continue.

   Continue the story you have received, again including one of the captions and one sequence expression.

I didn't notice anything unusual about her at first.

I found an empty space and parked the car.

At first, he drove quite normally.

An old man in a straw hat was sitting in the café drinking whisky.

From the outside, the house looked deserted.

Stretched out on the floor was a large Alsatian dog.

Focus on Form

In cold blood

It was 11 am on 22 July, 1956. The phone rang. It was a Mrs Mary Roberts, reporting the murder of her husband Jay, in their remote lakeside cabin about two hours from Chicago.

I drove out.

It was clear what had happened. He had been reading the paper when …

The smell was dreadful. When I looked at the date on the newspaper, I knew why. …

The wife had a watertight alibi. …

The study was in a terrible mess. Someone …

Outside, there were two large footprints. It looked as if …

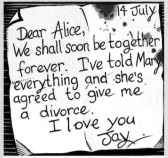

There was a letter in the dead man's pocket. Suddenly I realised a lot of things. …

I phoned the lab. An hour later, my suspicions were confirmed. It wasn't Jay Roberts' blood on the newspaper. I drove out and arrested Mary Roberts for murder.

She had been fiendishly clever. She had, of course, killed her husband before …

The next day, …

On her return, she …

Then she had phoned the police.

1 Flashbacks

Read the story, and use the information in the pictures to fill in the missing parts.

Can you solve the mystery?

2 Reporting verbs

> Don't take too much money with you if you're going out at night.

> I'll pay for the damage.

> If you don't get off my land immediately, I'll call the police.

> Well actually, it was me who left the front door unlocked.

> It was you who broke the window, wasn't it?

> Don't forget to take the key with you will you?

Match these remarks with the sentence beginnings below. Complete the sentences, to report what the people said.

a He threatened …	d They warned …
b He admitted …	e She offered …
c She accused …	f He reminded …

3 Two kinds of relative clause

> **Defining relative clauses**
> The man *who lives next door to me* is a novelist. He wrote the book *(that) I'm reading at the moment.*
>
> **Non-defining relative clauses**
> James Knott, *who lives next door to me*, is a novelist. He wrote 'Under the Stars', *which I'm reading at the moment.*

Look at the examples. What's the difference between defining and non-defining relative clauses? Think about

– meaning
– relative pronouns
– commas.

Now combine these pairs of sentences, using a suitable relative clause.

a My friend Laura has just got a part in a film. I share a flat with her.
b Last night I met a man. His parents were trapeze artists.
c The letter hasn't arrived yet. You sent it last week.
d They spend all their time playing with their new computer. They keep it in the kitchen.
e Giant pandas live entirely on bamboo shoots. They're in danger of extinction.

6 Do it yourself

1 Instructions

1 Here are some instructions for using a variety of products.
What kind of products do you think they are?

Add boiling water.

LIGHT END
OF FUSE
AT ARM'S
LENGTH.

Wait until
surfaces are touch dry
(about 15 minutes).

Lather, rinse, repeat if desired.

Double click on
Installer icon.

Stir well with a broad
stirring stick.

Wait until green light
indicates flash is ready.

Turn dial to select programme required.

The instructions below come before and after the ones in the illustrations.
Can you reconstruct the full set of instructions for each product?

a Ensure that all surfaces are free from grease
   and dust …
   … Apply two coats with brush or pad.

b Place upright in bottle or tube …
   … Stand well clear.

c Place bag in cup …
   … Leave for 5 minutes to bring out the full
   flavour.

d Insert Disk 1 into floppy drive …
   … Follow on-screen instructions.

e Apply sparingly to both surfaces …
   … Position together accurately and then
   press hard.

f Gently massage into wet hair and scalp …
   … For best results, follow with Organics
   Conditioner.

g Fill dispenser with detergent …
   … Press power switch to start washing cycle.

h Depress shutter button half way …
   … Depress shutter button fully to take
   picture.

2 What differences do you notice between the language
of written instructions and normal spoken English?

Choose one set of instructions.
How would you explain to a friend what to do?
Add any details you like.

2 What needs doing?

1 What's wrong with the things in the pictures?
Use words from the box to help you.

crack	come off
leak	missing
peel	rotten
stain	damp
tear	puncture

What do you think needs
doing to put things right?

🔲 Now listen to the
suggestions in the recording.
Are they the same as yours?

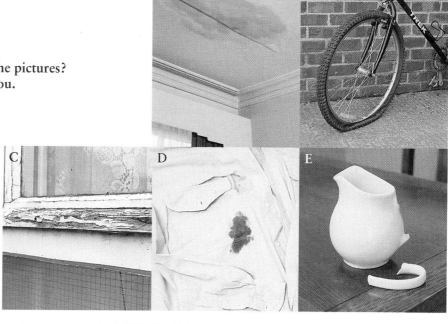

2 Work in pairs. Find out which of you is more practical. Which of the jobs would
you be able to do yourself, and which would you get someone else to do?

3 Creative cooking

What do you do when friends turn up unexpectedly and you haven't done any shopping?
Answer: do the best you can with what you've got! This new series offers imaginative recipes that require only the
most ordinary of ingredients. This week, a delicious combination of tuna, apple and brandy!

BAKED TUNA *and* APPLE FLAMBÉ

What you've got

1 onion	1 apple	some stale bread
1 tin tuna	100 g butter	a bottle of brandy

First ....1........ the onion and the apple. Thinly ....2........ the onion, and ....3........ the apple into small pieces. ....4........ the butter in a pan, and ....5........ the onion gently in the butter until it begins to turn yellow. Then ....6........ half a cup of water. Bring to the boil and leave to ....7........ for a few minutes. ....8........ the tuna and the chopped apple, and ....9........ thoroughly. Put the mixture in an ovenproof dish. ....10........ breadcrumbs over the top, and ....11........ in a hot oven for 30 minutes or until it is golden brown. Warm a small glass of brandy and ....12........ it over the baked tuna. Set light to it, and ....13........ immediately.

1 Fill the gaps in the recipe with verbs from the box.

sprinkle	serve	fry	melt
simmer	slice	add	pour
bake	chop	peel	stir

Would you eat baked tuna and apple flambé?

2 Work in groups.
On a piece of paper, write a list of ingredients
suitable for the magazine series.

Give your list to another group, who will write a recipe for you.

What do you think of the result?

4 They did it themselves

READING

1 **Read through the article quickly, and find answers to these questions.**

 a What does Andrea Gordon's invention do?
 b How did she start thinking about it?
 c How does it work?
 d What was the main problem in producing it?
 e Is she going to give up acting?

ME AND MY GIZMO
Socking it to 'em

ACTRESS Andrea Gordon has got little feet coming out of her ears. At least, she has since she turned her hand to invention. She is the proud inventor of a foot-shaped, plastic device which keeps your pairs of socks together in the washing machine.

So how did the idea occur to her for such an important breakthrough in domestic technology? Archimedes would have approved of her answer.

'It was just a string of little coincidences,' says Andrea modestly. 'A group of us were having dinner after working all day in the studio, and we got talking about universal problems like traffic congestion and lost socks.

'One of the actors said he had ended up taking his washing machine apart to retrieve a sock and had to spend all day Saturday putting it back together again.' The problem was defined.

'I just got thinking, "Why doesn't somebody invent a peg or something just to keep them together?"' Indeed. 'I was just thinking about it and a couple of hours later I was drying up the dishes and I put the tea-towel in one of those plastic grips you get.' Eureka!

'It seemed so obvious that it would work,' she confesses, 'that I was sure someone must have thought of it already.' Nobody had. 'So when I lost an expensive £20 silk sock, that was what finally persuaded me to go for it.'

BUT WAS THIS a real problem for which people really needed a solution? MIA Marketing thought so, and took on the idea.

'I don't set out to solve the world's problems,' says Andrea, 'but at least it's one annoying little thing out of the way. This invention is going to reduce stress levels, so I've done my bit.'

Once the real need for this gizmo had been established, the process of testing began. 'It wasn't easy,' remembers Andrea. 'The first plastic cracked.' They eventually settled on the more expensive thermoplastic polyurethane elastoma, a plastic that retains its shape in boiling water, and even in the rough and tumble world of sock-washing.

NOW LITTLE FEET are available from major shops at £1.95 for a pack of five. According to the advertising blurb on the packet, they are 'suitable for men's, women's and children's socks' and they come in different colours for 'all the family'.

SO WILL THIS breakthrough change Andrea's life? Will she be turning down acting work to become a full-time inventor? 'Acting is what I do,' she insists. 'But I'm glad I saw this idea through. A lot of people have ideas and they don't do anything about them, or they are put off by people not listening to them.'

So now you know – marketing people will listen to anything that might make money.

William Mayes

2 **Now read the article more carefully.**
 What is the significance of the following?

 – the studio
 – a tea-towel
 – a silk sock
 – MIA Marketing
 – stress levels
 – elastoma

3 These conversational expressions appear in the article.
   What do you think they mean?

   a ... she *turned her hand to* invention
   b ... and we *got talking*
   c ... he had *ended up* taking ...
   d I just *got thinking* ...
   e ... persuaded me to *go for it*
   f ... and *took on* the idea
   g ... so I've *done my bit*
   h ... they eventually *settled on* ...
   i ... I *saw* this idea *through*
   j ... they are *put off* by people not listening ...

4 Do you think the style of the article is

   – serious and analytical?
   – enthusiastic and persuasive?
   – negative and critical?
   – amusing and ironical?

   Find examples from the article to support your point of view.

LISTENING

1 Here are eight statements about a dish called *tarte flambée*, **and a new restaurant which will soon be serving it.**

   a 200 years ago, people had a good reason for cooking tarte flambée.
   b It's similar to pizza.
   c It's different from pizza.
   d People will like it.
   e It's not expensive.
   f It's quick to cook.
   g Eating in La Tarte Flambée will be very different from eating in a formal gastronomic restaurant.
   h It will also be more fun than other fast food restaurants.

   Read the publicity material. Which of the statements does it help to explain?

2 [cassette icon] **Now listen to the restaurant's owner, Philippe Roy, talking about his new restaurant. What does he say that helps to explain the eight statements?**

3 **What would you say are the three main attractions of La Tarte Flambée?**

DISCUSSION

Do you think either Little Feet or La Tarte Flambée will be a commercial success? Why / Why not?

Your teacher will tell you how well they were doing a year after they were launched. Did they do as well/badly as you expected?

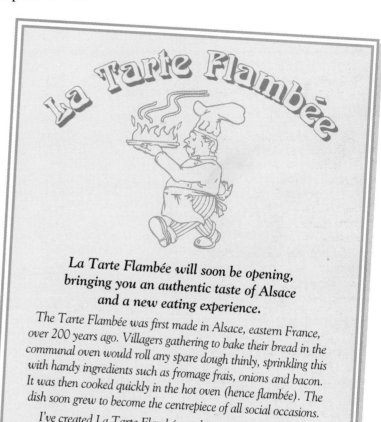

La Tarte Flambée

La Tarte Flambée will soon be opening, bringing you an authentic taste of Alsace and a new eating experience.

The Tarte Flambée was first made in Alsace, eastern France, over 200 years ago. Villagers gathering to bake their bread in the communal oven would roll any spare dough thinly, sprinkling this with handy ingredients such as fromage frais, onions and bacon. It was then cooked quickly in the hot oven (hence *flambée*). The dish soon grew to become the centrepiece of all social occasions.

I've created La Tarte Flambée so that you too can enjoy a taste of Alsace in a warm and friendly atmosphere. Prices will be very reasonable – in fact you can enjoy a traditional tarte flambée and a glass of wine for only £5!

Philippe Roy

Study pages

Grammar study: -ing forms

1 Verbs and nouns

Look at the words in italics. What's the difference
between those in A and those in B?
What's the connection between them?

| A | *Nicotine* is bad for your health.
I enjoy *music*.
Thank you for the *present*. |
| B | *Smoking* is bad for your health.
I enjoy *walking*.
Thank you for *inviting* me. |

Complete these sentences with -*ing* forms instead of
the nouns in italics, so they have roughly the same
meaning.

a He's very good at *maths*.
b He wastes all his money on *the lottery*.
c She went out without *her coat*.
d *Factory work* can be very boring.

2 Verb + -ing

| admit | consider | involve | risk |
| avoid | deny | miss | suggest |

All the verbs in the box can be followed by -*ing*
forms. Fill the gaps with suitable verbs.

a He .... being in the building at the time, but
.... shooting the security guard.
b Her job .... travelling all over the world.
c I was about to cook lunch when he ....
getting a take-away instead.
d It's great that the children can read now,
although I really .... reading them a
bedtime story.
e The Stock Market isn't for me. I don't want to
.... losing all my money.
f Let's go now to .... getting stuck in the
traffic.
g Now we can afford it, we're .... buying a
new car.

Now complete these sentences.

a The walls are a bit thin, so could you avoid ...
b I love living in the country, but I miss ...
c Learning a language involves ...
d I'm tired of living alone. I'm considering ...

3 Preposition + -ing

-*ing* forms often follow verbs and phrases with
prepositions. Here are some examples:

> I'm thinking *of starting* my own business.
> Are you accusing me *of cheating*?
> He's not very good *at making* polite conversation.

Fill the gaps in these sentences. Include a
preposition and an -*ing* form.

a At last she succeeded .... Mount Everest.
b I absolutely insist .... the meal.
c Would you be interested .... the Folk
Festival?
d He's not used .... on his own.
e They tried to prevent us .... the building.
f He never forgave her .... his Persian carpet.
g I prefer watching videos .... the cinema.
h She's really looking forward .... school.

4 Other people's actions

Look at the examples. Which use a passive form?

> I don't mind *you correcting my mistakes*.
> I don't like *people smoking in the house*.
> I can't stand *being laughed at*.
> I don't mind *you phoning me at work*.
> I hate *being called 'Miss'*.

Imagine these things happening to a young child.
How do you think she feels about them?

– her parents give her sweets
– she gets bullied at school
– her parents often go out in the evening
– people pat her on the head

Now think about your own childhood. What did
you like/dislike people doing?

5 Infinitive or -ing?

Look at these pairs of examples. What do they tell
you about the verbs *like*, *remember*, *forget* and *try*?

1 *a* I like singing in the shower.
   b I like to pay my bills as soon as I receive them.
2 *a* I don't remember seeing you here before.
   b I must remember to post that letter.
3 *a* I'll never forget shaking Mick Jagger by the
        hand.
   b I forgot to write down their telephone
        number.
4 *a* We tried to open the door, but it was locked.
   b – I can't get the video to work.
        – Why don't you try changing the plug?

Choose the best answer.

a – He won't help me.
     – Well, have you tried *asking/to ask* him?
b I remember *riding/to ride* on a steam train when
     I was eight.
c Don't forget *ringing/to ring* me when you get
     home.
d I tried *lighting/to light* a fire, but the wood was
     damp.
e Cats like *keeping/to keep* themselves very clean.

Language awareness: British and US English

1 *a* One of the most obvious differences between British and US English is in common vocabulary. Can you match these American words with their British equivalents? Use a dictionary to help you.

sidewalk	fall	closet	drapes
line	freeway	garbage	
truck	yard	elevator	candy

lift	rubbish	sweets	motorway
pavement	garden	wardrobe	
curtains	lorry	autumn	queue

b [cassette icon] You will hear a short anecdote about an Englishman visiting the US.

– What did the Englishman offer to do?
– Why did his hosts laugh?

Here are some other words that mean different things in British and US English. Find out what they mean in each.

a pants   *c* a bill   *e* (potato) chips
b a subway *d* a purse

2 Some words are spelt differently. Here are some British English words. How would an American spell them? Use a dictionary if necessary.

a honour; colour   *c* travelled; marvellous
b centre; theatre

3 There are also some minor differences in grammar. Here are some sentences in American English. How would they be different in British English?

a I saw my friend Sally on the weekend.
b The President was in Moscow Tuesday.
c Don't forget to write me.
d He loves to read in bed.
e I already boiled the water, but I didn't make the coffee yet.
f I found London very strange at first, but now I've gotten used to it.

[cassette icon] You will hear an American talking about the differences. Listen and check your answers.

Pronunciation: rising and falling tones

1 [cassette icon] Look at these conversations and listen to B's replies. Where does her voice *rise* and where does it *fall*? What is the difference between the two replies?

1 A I've arranged to see Sue on Tuesday.
  B / But our meeting's / on Tuesday. /

2 A See you at the meeting on Friday.
  B / But our meeting's / on Tuesday. /

2 [cassette icon] Listen to these conversations. Decide which sections of B's replies have a *rising tone* and which have a *falling tone*.

1 A I'm going to Moscow.
  B / You might see Boris / in Moscow. /

2 A When are you going to Malaysia?
  B / I leave here / on Friday. /

3 A I like your jacket. Where did you get it?
  B / I bought it / in Paris. /

4 A Is this Don's bag?
  B / The one on the left / is Don's. /

5 A How did you learn to speak German?
  B / I learnt German / at school. /

Now try saying them yourself.

3 Look at B's replies in these conversations. Which sections do you think will have a rising tone, and which will have a falling tone?

1 A Did you do much over the holiday?
  B / We just stayed at home / most of the time. /

2 A What did you do at the weekend?
  B / On Saturday / I went shopping / and on Sunday / I went for a walk. /

3 A What's it like living on your own?
  B / I really enjoy it / most of the time / but it does get a bit lonely / sometimes. /

4 A Are you still playing football these days?
  B / When I'm working / I don't get much time / but when I'm on holiday / I often play. /

[cassette icon] Now listen and see if you were right.

7 Working it out

1 Mysteries of the universe

must, might, can't • infinitive forms

1 Read the texts and choose opinions that are closest to your own.
Give reasons for your opinions.

A

Many people are convinced that there is life elsewhere in the universe. Scientists are busy searching for evidence of other forms of life, in the form of radio signals, but so far have found no trace.

> There must/might/can't be life elsewhere in the universe

B

Every year, a number of people claim that they were abducted by aliens. They usually say that they were taken on board an alien spaceship for scientific experiments and released a few hours later.

> Aliens must/might/can't be abducting human beings on a regular basis.

C

© Roswell Footage 1995

This still is from a film claiming to show an autopsy on a dead alien who crash-landed in the Nevada Desert in 1947. The owner says it was kept secret for years by the US Military. But is it a fake?

> Aliens must/might/can't have landed on Earth.

D

A number of huge shapes were drawn on the ground in Nazca, Peru, around 2000 years ago. Since they are visible only from the air, some believe they were drawn by aliens.

> The Nazca lines must/might/can't have been drawn by aliens.

2 Now read the article *Life Elsewhere?* on page 93. What opinions does the writer have?
Have you changed any of your opinions after reading the article?

2 Otherwise …

2nd & 3rd conditionals

1 Match the deductions and the reasons. What's the connection between each pair?

They can't be in.		… they would have taken the car.
They can't have recognised us.		… the lights would be on.
They must be expecting guests.		… they would have waved.
They must have got stuck in traffic.	Otherwise …	… they'd be here by now.
They must be on expenses.		… they wouldn't be travelling first class.
They can't have gone far.		… the house wouldn't be so tidy.

2 Give reasons for these deductions. Begin each reason with *Otherwise* …

– They must be hard up.   – They must have moved.   – They must be very happily married.

– They can't be hard up.   – They can't have moved.   – They can't be very happily married.

Read out some of your reasons. Can other students guess which deductions they go with?

3 How do you picture it?

look • seem • appear

1 Look at this painting, which is called *Regarding Soup*, and think about these questions.

– How old do you think the woman is?
– Who do you think the man is?
– What about the other figure?
– What's the significance of the soup?
– What is the woman doing?
– Why do you think they're wearing sunglasses?
– What do you think the picture is trying to say?

You will hear two people talking about the picture. How do they answer the questions? Do you agree with them?

Now listen again. How do the speakers use these words?

– look
– seem
– appear

2 Work in groups. Look at the painting on page 94, which is by the same artist.

How do you interpret it?

© 1994 Gabriella Roth

4 Why do they do it?

1 Why do people gamble, even though they know that they're more likely to lose money than win? Here are four different people's explanations. Read them and note down all the expressions used for talking about *reason* and *purpose*.

A I think people gamble for many reasons, but one is so as to bring some excitement into their lives. Buying a lottery ticket, for example, gives you something to look forward to, and you can have a lot of fun imagining what you would do if you won.

C People who gamble a lot probably do it for the same reason that people take drugs – it gives them some kind of a 'high'. The problem is, of course, that this sort of gambling can easily become addictive.

D Well, I play cards for money sometimes, and it's just a way of having a good time with my friends. We get together and have a nice evening – we only play for small amounts of money, so there's not much risk in it.

B The most obvious reason why people gamble is in order to make money – even if you know you may not win, there's always a chance that you will. And for many people that's the only way they could ever make a lot of money.

2 Choose one of the questions below that interests you, and make a few notes of your own opinion. Then ask two or three other people in the class what they think, and make notes of what they say.

- Why do people start smoking?
- Why do people become politicians?
- Why do people hunt wild animals?
- Why do people go sky-diving?
- Why do people fast?
- Why do people enjoy watching violent films?
- Why do people run marathons?
- Why do people become vegetarians?
- Why do people take drugs?
- Why do people keep large dogs as pets?

3 Put the opinions you have collected together in a connected series of short paragraphs, like the example below.

There are various reasons why gambling is so popular. The most obvious reason why people gamble is in order to make money – even if you know you may not win, there's always a chance that you will. And for many people winning money from gambling is the only way they could ever make a lot of money.

Another reason people gamble is to bring some excitement into their lives. Buying a lottery ticket, for example, gives you something to look forward to, and you can have a lot of fun imagining what you would do if you won.

For most people, gambling is just a way of having a good time – for example, getting together with friends and playing cards for small amounts of money can be an enjoyable way of spending an evening.

But people who gamble a lot probably do it for the same reason that people take drugs – it gives them some kind of a 'high'. The problem is, of course, that serious gambling can easily become addictive and there's a real danger of it ruining your life.

Focus on Form

1 Must, might & can't

Rewrite these sentences using *must*, *might* **or** *can't*.

a Perhaps they're having lunch in the canteen.
b She was obviously driving too fast.
c I'm sure you were surprised.
d You didn't enjoy that much, I'm quite sure.
e It's possible that he's been kidnapped.
f Surely there's some explanation.
g Surely you don't mean that!
h I'm quite sure you're joking.

Now complete the following using *must*, *might* **or** *can't*.

a ... – you haven't slept for 24 hours.
b Their phone's engaged, so ...
c ... because her passport's still in the drawer.
d If they don't answer the door, try looking round the back – ...
e His fingerprints aren't on the gun, so ...

2 'Unreal' conditionals

Look at these sentences. Which refer to

– the present?
– the past?
– both present and past?

a If you had measles, you'd be covered in spots.
b If she'd lived in France, she'd know what Ça va means.
c If you really loved me, you wouldn't have said that.
d If he'd been driving carefully, he would have seen them coming.

Student A: **Choose an item from Box A and change it into the first half of an** *If ...* **sentence.**
Student B: **Choose an item from Box B to continue the sentence.**

Example:

A If they had a mobile phone ...
B ... we could have got in touch with them.

Box A

1 Unfortunately they haven't got a mobile phone.
2 I'm a very polite person.
3 I'm sure they're not on holiday.
4 It's lucky you jumped out of the way.
5 Of course they like us.
6 She's just won the lottery.
7 I'm sure he's at home.
8 You weren't listening to what I told you.

---

3 Seem & appear

Read the text, and talk about the woman, using *seem* **and** *appear*.

Examples:

She doesn't appear to have a job.
She seems to have had a tragedy in her life.

I don't know my next door neighbour, but I've noticed a few things about her ...
　　She wears a wedding ring, but hers is the only name on the door. A woman driving a Porsche often comes to visit her, and I've heard them talking together in Spanish.
　　I've never seen her go to work in the morning, but she's always on the phone, and she gets a lot of mail, much of it from Mexico.
　　Recently she put extra locks on her front door, and I've often heard her crying at night.
　　She has pictures of Moscow on her walls, but when I said 'Zdravstvuytye' to her the other day, she looked at me completely blankly.

4 The five senses

Fill the gaps using *look*, *sound*, *taste*, *smell* **or** *feel*, **adding** *like* **or** *as if* **where necessary.**

a Your socks .... rotten eggs.
b You .... you've got a cold.
c I can't eat this. It .... too salty.
d I'm not sure what it is. It .... some kind of prehistoric tool.
e My head .... someone's hitting it with a hammer.

Now complete these remarks.

a Are you sure this is cotton? It feels ...
b Now that you've shaved your beard off, you look ...
c Euurgh! Do you call this soup? It tastes ...
d What on earth is going on next door? It sounds ...
e I wouldn't eat that meat. It smells ...

Box B

a You weren't run over.
b He's left the front door open.
c We couldn't get in touch with them.
d That's why he asked her to marry him.
e That's why you don't know what to do.
f That's why they invited us to their party.
g They haven't sent us a postcard.
h I didn't tell her what I really thought of her.

---

8 | In the market-place

1 The right career?

Careers guidance questionnaire

1 Which of these areas can you see yourself working in? Tick the boxes.

☐ business
✓ arts/entertainment
✓ education
✓ health and welfare
✓ media

☐ industry
☐ science/technology
☐ the environment
✓ politics/public life
☐ service industries

Other: ....

2 How true are these statements of you? Give yourself a mark out of five.

3 I don't mind hard physical work.
5 I enjoy working with my hands.
3 I enjoy solving problems.
5 I'm a good listener.
2 I'm good with figures.
4 I have a good artistic sense.
5 I'm a good communicator.

3 Do you have any particular skills or leisure interests?

Painting and decorating
Painting pictures
I speak Spanish and German
Sports – both watching and playing
Listening to music, socialising, walking

4 What are/were your favourite subjects at school?

Art, English, Sport

....

....

5 What do you expect from a job? Give each of these a mark out of five.

3 prospects for promotion
5 the power to take your own decisions
5 contact with other people
3 a good salary
4 the chance to travel
5 long holidays
3 being able to leave the job behind you when you go home

6 How true are these statements of you? Give each a mark out of 5.

4 I get on with other people.
3 I don't mind taking orders.
3 I need to be my own boss.
4 I go crazy if I do the same thing for too long.
3 I can cope when things get tough.
3 I like to look smart.
2 I can keep smiling – however I'm feeling.
4 I'm punctual.

1 Read the completed careers guidance questionnaire.
Do you see this person as

– a boss or an employee?
– working in an organisation or self-employed?
– having a safe, steady job or doing something more adventurous?

Think of a specific job for the person.

2 Now fill in the questionnaire yourself (there's a copy on page 95) and give it to the teacher.

Work with a partner. The teacher will give you two completed questionnaires.
Look at them, and suggest two or three suitable jobs for the writers.

Now look at the suggestions that have been made for you.
What do you think of them?

---

2 Success story

You will hear someone telling the story of a company called *Future Publishing*. Here are some of the things the person says. Put them in the order you think you will hear them.

a He set up a company called *Future Publishing*.
b Over the next eight years, their turnover rose by 90% a year.
c They kept adding new magazine titles.
d Chris Anderson was working for a company that produced a home computer magazine.
e They launched their own computer magazine.
f The next issue made a profit.
g They managed to pay off the bank loan in just three months.
h He was sacked.
i He decided to sell the company.
j They took on more staff.
k They didn't sell enough copies to break even.
l They took out a bank loan of £15,000.

 Now listen to the recording. Were you right?

3 Legal, decent, honest, truthful

1 This advertisement was banned in Britain after people complained about it to the Advertising Standards Authority (ASA). Why do you think it was banned?

The ASA provides rules for companies advertising their products in Britain. Here are some of them.

a No advertisement should cause fear or anxiety without good reason.

b Advertisements should contain nothing that is likely to cause serious or widespread offence, particularly on the grounds of race, religion or sex.

c Advertisements should not make children feel inferior or unpopular for not buying the advertised product.

d Advertisements should not imply a link between smoking and social, sexual, romantic or business success.

e Advertisers should not unfairly attack other businesses or their products.

f Advertisements should not suggest that alcohol is the main reason for the success of a party or event.

On pages 96–7 there are some ideas for advertisements. Some of them break the rules above, and some break other ASA rules. What do you think the other rules might be?

2 Are there any advertisements you've seen recently that you object to? What don't you like about them? Do you think they should be banned?

4 Dirty money

READING

1 The fax opposite was received by a small company in London in early 1995.
Use the questions below to help you read and understand it.

   a Who is Bernard Sithole?
   b How old is he?
   c How did he get hold of the $5 million?
   d Where is the money now?

   e What does he want to do with the $5 million?
   f Why is his position 'sensitive'?
   g What does he want the recipient of the fax to do?
   h What would the recipient get from the deal?

2 Find phrases in the text that mean:

   a after working for many years
   b a business that operates successfully
   c a partner from abroad

   d helping me
   e make sure I can retire safely
   f the deal which will help us both.

DISCUSSION

Imagine that you are the Managing Director of the company that received the fax.
How would you respond? Why? What would you expect to happen if you took up
the offer?

LISTENING

🎞 You will hear part of a radio programme about companies receiving faxes like
the one you have just read. The recording is in two parts.

Part 1

1 Who is Alex Clarke?

2 What differences are there between this offer and the one you read about? Think about:

   – who sent the fax
   – how much they want to transfer
   – why they want to transfer the money

   – what they want him to do
   – how much money he could make

3 What did he decide to do? Why?

Part 2

4 Does the police inspector think Alex Clarke did the right thing? Why?

5 Here are key words from three points the inspector makes. How do they fit together?

   a bank details – headed
     notepaper – transfer –
     bank account
   b oil company – $1.5
     million – £700,000
   c charities – died – death
     duties

6 What does the presenter
  advise listeners to do if
  they receive a similar fax?
  Is that what you decided
  to do?

URGENT & CONFIDENTIAL

ATTN: The President/Managing Director.   Tel/Fax ████████

Dear Sir,

INTRODUCTION & BIO-DATA
I am Prince Bernard Sithole, Minister in charge of Contracts in the ████████ Oil Corporation. My position is very sensitive. I am married with children and hold degrees in public administration and business studies. I am due for retirement any moment from now, after many years in service.

REASON(S) FOR CONTACTING YOU
I urgently need your assistance in providing me with a safe and reliable bank account with full details, viz: Name and Address of Bank, Telephone, Telex and Fax Number anywhere in the world where I can transfer the sum of **5 Million** U.S. Dollars. The purpose of the transfer is to take care of my retirement by investing in a viable business.

NATURE OF BUSINESS
The above sum (5 Million U.S.D.) arises from various contracts I have awarded since I have been in this post. For the present, I have arranged for the money to be kept in a coded bank account with the National Bank of ████████ until I am able to find a reliable overseas partner to whom it can be transferred. Once the payment has been approved, you might be required to visit our country to sign the necessary papers.

SHARING THE FUNDS
30% will go to you for making available to me a company/personal account number, giving me your assistance and keeping strictly to the rules of this transaction until the money has been transferred. 10% will be used to cover expenses: obtaining vital documents, tips, trips made by both parties, phone/fax bills, hotel bills, taxes and bank charges. 60% will be shared between me and a few colleagues of mine whose help will be needed to complete the transaction.

OTHER RELEVANT DETAILS
Everything about this transaction is real. The money is clean. After putting in so many years in service, it is only normal for me to take steps to secure my period in retirement. I have worked very hard to make this transaction possible, which means that it means a lot to me, and hopefully, with a little help from you, everything will be settled in just a matter of weeks. It will come to mean a lot to you too as we meet in your country to celebrate the closing of the deal.

If you are interested in this mutual benefit, please contact me immediately at the above fax number and also complete the attached ████████ Oil Corporation **Payment Information** form.

Thank you for your kind understanding and co-operation in anticipation.

Yours sincerely,

Prince Bernard Sithole.

PRINCE BERNARD SITHOLE

Find out

1 A Write down a short list of games that you know how to play, and/or things that you know how to cook. Show it to B.

   B Choose an item from the list that interests you, and ask A to teach you how to do it.

2 Sit in groups. What's the most interesting/unusual painting or photo you've got at home? Describe it to the others.

   Which of the pictures you've heard about do you imagine you would like best?

3 Ask other students to tell you about

   – an advertisement they particularly like
   – an advertisement they particularly dislike.

   What is it that they like/dislike about them?

4 Find out if other students believe that

   – there's a monster in Loch Ness
   – Lord Lucan is still alive
   – the world is getting warmer.

   What reasons do they have?

Words

1 Imagine a house that has not been lived in for several years, and say what might be wrong with it. Think about

   the roof   windows   ceilings   wood

2 Add words to these lists.

   – note, notice, announcement …
   – grammar, vocabulary …
   – stir, roast, chop …

3 Imagine someone who knows nothing about *either* football *or* tennis. Think of five useful vocabulary items for them to learn, and explain what they mean.

4 In what situations might you

   – lose touch with someone?
   – make small talk?
   – make it up with someone?
   – take on staff?
   – go bankrupt?

Role-play

1 A You're going to be interviewed for one of these jobs. Think about what you'll say.

> Wanted: **NANNY** to look after three young children. Some cooking and cleaning. Driver's licence essential.
>
> Wanted: **ENGLISH TEACHER** to teach beginners. Training given, but experience an advantage.
>
> Wanted: **ACTORS/ACTRESSES** for small parts in a popular daytime soap. Good acting ability essential.

   B You're about to interview A. Think of some questions you will ask him/her.

   Now conduct the interview.

2 Choose one of these situations and improvise a conversation.

   – A accuses B of something.
   – A threatens B.
   – A offers B something he/she doesn't want.

   Now report what was said to other students.

3 A You're just leaving school/college and you can't decide what kind of career to take up. Ask B for some advice.

   B You're a careers adviser. Try to help A decide on a career.

Writing

1 A B is going to look after your flat while you're away. Leave a note saying what you want him/her to do, and explaining how to use e.g. the washing machine, cooker, TV.

   B Read A's note, then imagine you've now been staying in A's flat. Write a note to leave for when he/she comes back home.

2 A Write five or six sentences about the history of your country. Include at least three factual mistakes.

   B Read what A has written. See if you can find the mistakes, and correct them.

3 Why do you think so many men are keen on football, but so few women are? Write a few sentences about it.

Talking points

Prepare a short talk (about one minute) using one of these pictures as a starting point.

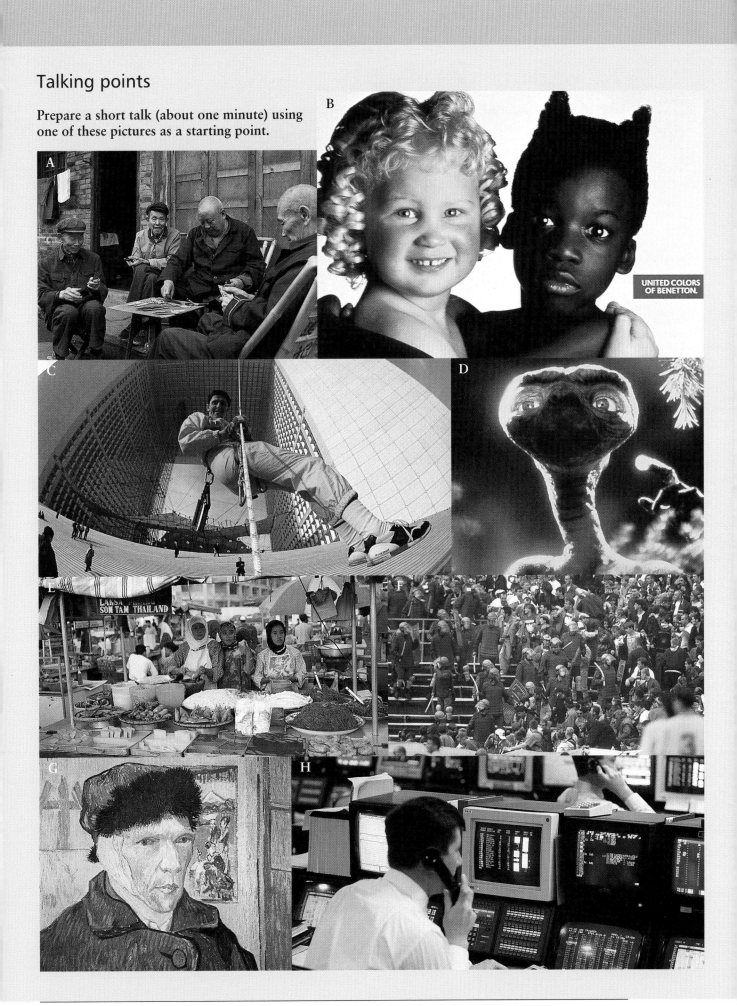

9 Possibilities

1 If we carry on like this …

will & would

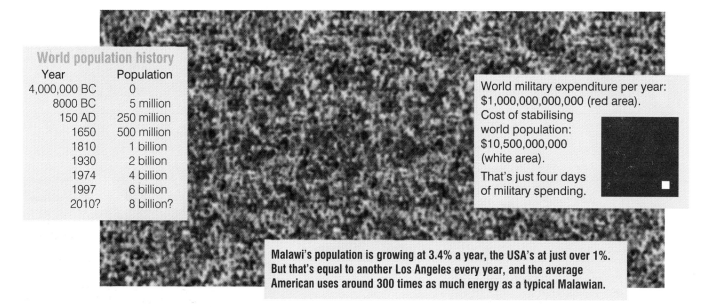

World population history

Year	Population
4,000,000 BC	0
8000 BC	5 million
150 AD	250 million
1650	500 million
1810	1 billion
1930	2 billion
1974	4 billion
1997	6 billion
2010?	8 billion?

World military expenditure per year: $1,000,000,000,000 (red area). Cost of stabilising world population: $10,500,000,000 (white area).

That's just four days of military spending.

Malawi's population is growing at 3.4% a year, the USA's at just over 1%. But that's equal to another Los Angeles every year, and the average American uses around 300 times as much energy as a typical Malawian.

1 Here are three opinions about the problem of world population. Read each one and summarise the main point in one sentence. Which opinion do you agree with most?

A

If we carry on like this, the world will eventually run out of energy, clean water, food and land. Some of the poorest countries will soon have nuclear weapons, and will probably use them, as resources become scarce and wars begin to break out.

If disaster is to be avoided, we must take action now to reduce the size of the world's population.

There is much the richer nations could do to encourage people to have smaller families. For example, if they gave all women in developing countries $25 a month until the birth of their third child, this would double or triple family incomes, and most women would decide to stop at two children, so as to keep receiving the money.

B

The problem is not that there are too many people in the world, but that we have not yet developed ways of meeting their needs. The world has faced many other challenges in the past, and found ways of dealing with them – indeed, progress is made precisely because there are problems to be solved.

There have already been spectacular increases in food production to meet the demands of rising populations, and as new problems arise, so solutions will be found for them.

What is not acceptable is for rich nations to tell poor people that they're not allowed to have children. If we continue to interfere in their affairs, we will only cause suffering and resentment.

C

The main reason that poor people have a lot of children is that children represent money: they can get jobs or provide their parents with free labour.

So the answer to the population problem lies in development. If their prosperity can be increased, people will begin to have fewer children. This has already happened in most of Europe, and is happening at the moment in countries such as South Korea and Taiwan.

If the rich nations want this to happen, they must cancel the huge debts that are crippling many developing countries. This would release much-needed money for economic development, and the population problem would look after itself.

When do the writers use *will*, and when do they use *would*?

2 Write down your own suggestion for helping to solve the world population problem, and pass it to another group.

Look at the suggestion you have received. Do you think it's a good idea? Why do you think it would or wouldn't work?

2 It depends

depend (on) • indirect questions

1 Complete the sentence beginning *It depends ...* using the questions in the green bubbles.

2 What do the answers to these questions depend on? Have short conversations.

 a Do you think I could get a job as a taxi driver?
 b How long does it take to cook a steak?
 c What's the best place to eat around here?
 d Is Britain a good place to go on holiday?

 Now ask your partner a question of your own.

How much does it cost to get to India?

It depends ...

How old are you?

What time of year do you want to go?

Are you flying or going overland?

3 Playing it safe

Probability expressions

1 How safe do you think it is to walk around the streets of New York on your own? What do you think you should and shouldn't do?

Harlem

Central Park

Manhattan

 Now listen to a New Yorker talking about the city, and answer these questions.

 a Does he think New York is a dangerous place?
 b What does he say about
  – Harlem?   – what you should wear?
  – Central Park?   – how you should behave?
  – Manhattan?
 c Write four sentences using the structures in the table.

You're	almost certain likely unlikely very unlikely	to get mugged if you ...

2 Think about the city where you live (or near where you live).

 Is the situation similar to that in New York or very different?
 What advice would you give to a visitor?

4 Courses of action

1 Here are parts of three paragraphs, which are about three different topics. Can you reconstruct them? Write them down, adding punctuation where necessary.

> alternatively, you could try to find temporary work in a hotel or a pub

> that would be more expensive, but it would give you much more light and space

> either the government could call a general election now

> the easiest thing to do would be just to give the rooms a coat of paint

> you could quite easily find work as an au pair with an English family

> but you might find it difficult to get a work permit

> or else they could wait till next year and hope the economy improves

> in which case they would probably win with a small majority

> another possibility would be to knock down one of the walls

2 Here are some ideas in note form. Expand them into a short paragraph, beginning with the sentence given.

There are various things you could do with your money …

keep it in a bank account   buy a flat   invest in antiques

safest   good investment somewhere to live   rather risky?

3 Think of a topic you are familiar with, either in your own or your friends' lives or in your country, in which there are different possible courses of action. Make notes like those above. If you like, use one of these ideas:

choosing a present for someone

redecorating a room

deciding what to study

getting to know someone

improving the local environment

planning a holiday

improving sales

preventing crime

Show your notes to another student, and explain what they are about. If necessary, improve them or add to them.

Then expand them into a paragraph.

Focus on Form

1 will or would?

Look at the remarks below, and choose between *will* **and** *would*.

a I don't know why you never ask your father to help. The exercise *will/would* do him good, and *he'll/he'd* probably enjoy it.

b – She promised me that *she'll/she'd* phone as soon as she got home.
    – Don't worry. I'm sure *she'll/she'd* ring soon.

c I wish your friends *will/would* wipe their feet when they come in.

d If I were you, *I'll/I'd* take it back to the shop.

e *I'll/I'd* carry that for you, if you like.

f If the Government doesn't cut taxes before the next election, it certainly *won't/wouldn't* get re-elected. So I expect that's exactly what it *will/would* do.

g *Will/Would* you pick up a hitchhiker late at night? I certainly *won't/wouldn't*.

h You must be crazy going by bus. *It'll/It'd* take you hours. If you went by train, *you'll/you'd* get there much faster.

i I wonder if *we'll/we'd* still be friends in 20 years' time.

2 Dependency

Look at the example situation below, and complete the sentences.

Do you think it will be a bumpy flight?

It depends on   the weather.
                 what …

It depends on   how good the pilot is.
                 whether …

It depends on   how big the plane is.
                 the …

3 Probability expressions

Rewrite these sentences using … *certain to / likely to / unlikely to / very unlikely to* …

a Unless you book in advance, you've got very little chance of getting a table.

b I'm quite sure she'll be given the job.

c Don't worry – you probably won't tread on a scorpion.

d I expect there'll be a big crowd at the match tonight.

Now change these sentences so that they express your own opinion.

a The population of the world will decline over the next ten years.

b There is intelligent life elsewhere in the universe.

c Lord Lucan will be found soon.

d There will be package tours to the Moon by the year 2100.

e The Loch Ness Monster exists.

f If you smoke heavily, you'll die young.

Now use *It depends* … **to talk about the other two situations. Can you think of any other things the answer depends on?**

Do you think I'll pass my driving test?

Do you think it'll be a good party?

10 Life, the universe and everything

Branches of science

1 The words in this spidergram are all to do with astronomy.
   Can you explain the connections shown by the lines?

   Example: Galileo was a famous astronomer.
            Galileo designed his own telescope.

2 Look at the words below. What branch of science is each connected with?

Work in groups. Choose one of the words, and use it as the starting point for your own
spidergram. Brainstorm ideas together.

Present your spidergram to the rest of the class, and explain how the ideas are connected.

2 Science and the environment

1 Here are 12 true/false questions about science and the environment.
In pairs, decide what the answers are. Can you justify your answers?

ARE THESE STATEMENTS TRUE OR FALSE?
Write T (= True) or F (= False) against each one

1 All radioactivity is made by humans. ☐

2 Antibiotics kill bacteria, but not viruses. ☐

3 Astrology, the study of star signs, has some scientific truth. ☐

4 Human beings developed from earlier species. ☐

5 All man-made chemicals cause cancer if you eat enough of them. ☐

6 If someone is exposed to any amount of radioactivity, they are certain to die as a result. ☐

7 Some radioactive waste from nuclear power stations will stay dangerous for thousands of years. ☐

8 The greenhouse effect is caused by a hole in the Earth's atmosphere. ☐

9 Every time we use coal or oil or gas, we contribute to the greenhouse effect. ☐

10 All pesticides and chemicals used on food crops cause cancer in humans. ☐

11 Human beings are the main cause of plant and animal species dying out. ☐

12 Cars are not really an important cause of air pollution. ☐

Now listen and check your answers. How well did you do?

2 The questions you have just answered were originally used in a scientific survey.
Read about the results of the survey on page 98. How do the class results compare?

3 Beyond science?

Which of these things do you believe in? Mark your opinions in the grid.

It's not true	It's unlikely	I'm not sure	It's likely	It's definitely true	
					a Some people can communicate telepathically with each other.
					b The star sign you were born under affects your character.
					c Some people can tell the future by looking at cards.
					d Dreams can warn you about events before they happen.
					e People sometimes appear after death as ghosts or spirits.
					f Some people have magic powers that can help or harm others.
					g Some people can remember other lives they have lived in the past.
					h Some people can move objects by concentrating their minds on them.
					i Doing (or not doing) particular things can bring you good or bad luck.

Get together in groups, and compare your opinions.
If you disagree about any of the topics, explain why you think the way you do.

4 Science fiction

READING

The story opposite is in three parts. Read each part, and answer the questions.

PART 1

1 What is the relationship between the two men?
Why are they at the restaurant?
What's their connection to Miller?

2 What do these expressions tell us about the characters?
  – hideously obese
  – weasel-like
  – chortled
  – sluggishly made her way to the table
  – almost drooled

PART 2

1 What is Sloane's 'line of business'?
Why is Wilson so fat?
Why does Sloane fake a coughing fit?

2 What do these expressions mean?
  – what makes people tick
  – make this hit
  – Tell me another story
  – a total loony

PART 3

1 The last words of the story have been blanked out. What do you think they are?

2 Compare the words in italics with the synonyms in brackets. What extra meaning does the writer give by choosing these words?
  – *grabbed* his spoon (picked up)
  – the *monstrous* ice-cream creation (huge)
  – *slurping* the ice-cream *down* (eating)
  – it *clattered* (fell)
  – *splattered* nearby (splashed)
  – *fingering* his scar (touching)

LISTENING

You will hear a short story called *Zoo*. The story is in two parts.

1 Here are some of the elements in the first part. Try to imagine what the story is about.

the horse-spider
people of Kaan

ten thousand
people

six hours

Professor Hugo

a silver spaceship

barred cages

crowds of adults
and children

a dollar

the tri-city parking
area outside Chicago

23rd August

▭ Now listen to the first part of the story. How similar was it to your own ideas?

2 Here is the beginning of the second part of the story. Imagine how it might continue.

> Some two months and three planets later, the silver ship settled at last
> onto the familiar jagged rocks of Kaan …

▭ Now listen to the second part of the story.

3 Do you think the story is just for entertainment, or is the writer trying to tell us something?

Dessert

by Robert E. Rogoff

I

The waitress hovered around their table like a moth near a light. Finally, the hideously obese man waved her away.

'We're not ready to order yet,' he said. 'Come back in a few minutes.'

After the waitress departed, the weasel-like man with the scar across his face addressed his dining companion seated across the table from him. 'I can assure you as we sit here tonight that Miller is quite dead or will be within minutes.'

The obese man chortled. 'That is good news.' He turned his massive body and snapped his fingers. The chair groaned in protest.

The waitress sluggishly made her way to the table. 'What'll it be, honey?'

'I'm celebrating tonight,' said the obese man. 'Let me have a super duper hot fudge sundae with the works.' He almost drooled as he said this.

'And you, dearie?' the waitress asked scarface.

'Just coffee for me, dearie.' He grinned, showing a crooked row of teeth.

The fat man looked as serious as his Buddha-like face allowed. 'You'll receive the other ten thousand as per our agreement.'

II

Scarface grinned again and rubbed his hands together. 'Mr Wilson,' he said. 'In my line of business it pays to get to know what makes people tick. If you don't think it too presumptuous of me, I'd like to inquire –' He stopped abruptly as the waitress approached to fill his coffee cup. After she slowly melted away to the recesses of the dingy restaurant, he continued, 'I was wondering … just exactly why did you have me make this hit?'

Wilson picked up his fork and rubbed a finger across its tines. 'I suppose I can tell you. I don't care whether you believe me or not.'

'Why wouldn't I believe you?'

'Mr Sloane, the sundae I ordered was the first food in years not on my very strenuous 400-calorie-a-day diet.'

Sloane suppressed a smile. Tell me another story, he thought.

Wilson continued. 'Despite eating almost nothing since 1985, my weight has ballooned to over four hundred pounds. Last month I

discovered – never mind how – that Miller was eating for me. He ate the food and I gained the weight.'

Sloane laughed but covered it by faking a coughing fit. This guy was loony. But a job was a job. He would take anyone's money, even a total loony like Wilson.

III

The waitress appeared and placed the sundae before Wilson. Wilson grabbed his spoon and eagerly attacked the monstrous ice-cream creation. He lifted the first spoonful. 'Here's to the demise of Miller,' he said, slurping the ice-cream down.

Suddenly he dropped the spoon. It clattered to the formica table top. A clump of fudge-covered ice-cream splattered nearby.

'Are you okay?' asked Sloane.

'I don't feel too well,' moaned Wilson. A glazed look came into his eyes. 'Oh, no. Don't tell me …'

'What?'

'How did you do it?' he demanded. He was beginning to feel dizzy. And afraid.

'Do it?' asked Sloane, fingering his scar.

'How did you kill Miller?'

Sloane smiled crookedly. 'Nothin' to it, Mr Wilson.   '

Grammar study: time

1 Time expressions

Each of these sentences contains one mistake.
Can you correct them?

a I saw him on the day before yesterday.
b He made a lot of friends during he was at university.
c I've been learning English since four years.
d Would you like to come to dinner the next Friday?
e They were delayed during six hours.
f She hasn't woken up already.
g We bought this flat before six years.
h He's retiring in five year's time.
i We got to the airport until 5 o'clock.

2 Expressions with 'time'

Fill the gaps with expressions from the box.

in time	at the same time	for a time
on time	after a time	at the time
some time	from time to time	at one time

a I don't see them very often, but they drop in
  ....
b Her great grandfather emigrated to America
  .... during the 1890s.
c The train was exactly ....
d They were very happy at first, but .... they
  began to drift apart.
e It was a stupid thing to do, but I was only 15
  ....
f If you want to get there .... for the
  fireworks, you'd better hurry up.
g The trouble was, he thought he could ride a bike
  and read a comic ....
h .... , dinosaurs used to roam the Earth.
i I have to go away .... , but I promise I'll
  write to you every day.

3 Time periods

Look at these sentences. In Box A, the time period
begins and ends in the past. What about the others?

A	I was at university from 1987 to 1991, and then I worked as a courier for two years.
B	I've been collecting stamps for more than 20 years. I've had this album since I was ten.
C	I'm on holiday for another six weeks, but I'm only staying here until the end of August.
D	I'll be away for six days. I'll be in New York from the 3rd to the 5th, and then I'm going to visit my sister in California.

Write four things about yourself, one for each time
period.

4 Two types of activity

Look at the sentences in A and B.

A	We spent two hours watching the TV. We watched the TV for two hours. *(This is how we passed the time)*
B	It took us two hours to drive to Berlin. We drove to Berlin in two hours. *(This is something we achieved, and how long it took us)*

Rewrite these sentences, using structures from the
box.

a We sunbathed from two till three.
b I started cooking dinner at 5.30 and it was ready
  at 7.00.
c I started reading the report on Monday, but I
  didn't finish it till Friday.
d We started playing cards at 6.00 and we finished
  at midnight.
e I started university in 1990, and I got my degree
  five years later.

5 Two kinds of sequence

Why do the sentences in A use the Past simple tense
and the sentences in B use the Past perfect tense?

A	When he *sat* down, the chair collapsed. When I *read* his note, I knew it was all over. When the dentist *gave* me the injection, I felt a stab of pain.
B	When he'd *sat* down, he began to eat his lunch. When I'd *read* his note, I threw it on the fire. When the dentist *had given* me the injection, she smiled and said 'OK? Ready for the drill?'

Make up sensible endings for these sentences.

a When the plane landed ...
b When the plane had landed ...
c When I'd finished the housework ...
d When she walked into the room ...
e When the lights went out ...
f When he'd drunk the whisky ...

Language awareness: conversational fillers

1 In everyday conversation, people often use 'fillers' such as *um*, *well* and *sort of*. Can you think of any others?

🔊 You will hear three people talking about smoking. Note down the fillers the speakers use. Why do you think they use them? How necessary do you think they are?

2 We often use other expressions in conversation, which help to explain our attitude (e.g. *as far as I'm concerned*, *I think*).

🔊 You will hear people saying the things below. What else do they say? Listen for expressions which mean the same as the expressions in brackets.

A
> It was quite a small room, and it had yellow wallpaper with pictures of penguins on it.

(I'm trying to remember)

(I'm not sure)

B
> I've been very busy recently and I haven't had time to look at it.

(I'm telling you the truth)

(It's beyond my control)

C
> Let's organise a fancy dress party.

(I don't want to force this idea on you)

(Do you agree?)

D
> This government doesn't care about people's welfare at all. It's only interested in winning the next election.

(This is definitely true)

(This is my opinion)

3 Work with a partner. Choose one of the situations below, and improvise a conversation. Use any fillers you like to help you.
   a You are your partner's boss, and you're giving him/her the sack.
   b Tell your partner your earliest childhood memory.
   c What do you think is the most serious danger to mankind? Tell your partner about it.
   d Invite your partner to come and stay for the weekend.

Pronunciation: high key

1 🔊 You will hear this remark said twice:

Sonia and I have decided to get married.

What is the difference in the way the remark is said? What difference is there in meaning?

2 🔊 You will hear each of the remarks below said twice. Each time, decide which of the two implied meanings fits better, *a* or *b*.

1 He's decided to take up tennis.
   a He's been thinking about it for some time, so I'm not surprised
   b That's odd – he's not normally interested in sports.

2 She was asleep by eight o'clock.
   a It's her usual bedtime.
   b It was unusually early for her.

3 It tastes like asparagus soup.
   a That's what I think it is.
   b That's funny – I was expecting chicken soup.

4 He arrived late again this morning.
   a I'm not surprised – he's often late.
   b I wonder what's wrong – he's usually on time.

Now try saying the remarks yourself. See if other students can tell which meaning you are trying to express.

3 In each of these remarks the speaker is making a contrast. Underline the word where you think the speaker's voice will go *up*.

1 Although the prime minister is head of the government, it's the president that has most of the power.

2 I was expecting Paul to call, but when I answered the phone, it was Sarah.

3 Surprisingly, the tickets are cheaper than a year ago.

4 We went there on Saturday, not Friday.

5 Oh, I thought the French exam was easy. It was the maths exam I didn't like.

🔊 Now listen and see if you were right. Then practise saying the remarks yourself.

Evaluating

1 For better, for worse

1 Do you think things have got better or worse in your country over the last 20 years or so?
Which of these statements do you think are true?

a Children have | more / less | fun than they used to.

b Cities have become | dirtier. / cleaner.

c There's a | greater / smaller | variety of fruit and vegetables than there used to be.

d Young people used to behave | more / less | responsibly than they do now.

e Holidays have become | cheaper. / more expensive.

f There are | more / fewer | opportunities for women than there used to be.

g People are | more / less | prejudiced against foreigners than they used to be.

h More / Fewer | people wear perfume these days.

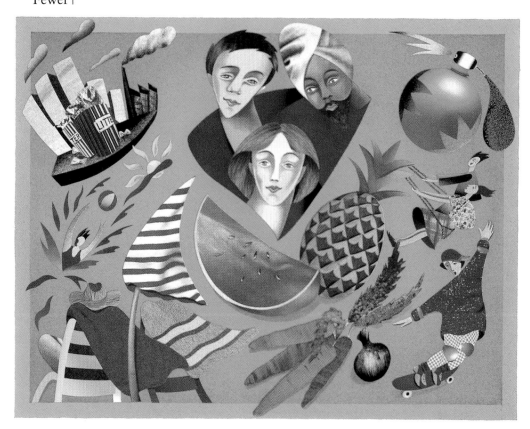

You will hear some people talking about how life in Britain has changed.
Do they say the same things as you? What other changes do they mention?

2 Now write two sentences of your own. Think of one change for the better in your
lifetime and one change for the worse.

2 What's the point?

1 Which of the expressions in the table are followed by *to* and which by *-ing*? Which of the expressions mean roughly the same?

2 What do you think about these things? Write three sentences like those in the table, and add a reason.

– going on a diet to lose weight
– taking part in political demonstrations
– keeping people alive who are in a terminal coma
– keeping old photos and letters
– giving money to help famine victims

Now find out if other people in the class agree with you. If they disagree, find out why.

It's a good idea It's worth(while) It's not worth There's no point in It's a waste of time It's not a good idea	giving money to beggars to give money to beggars

3 Gadgets

Causative verbs

1 Here are some pictures of gadgets taken from a book called *101 Unuseless Japanese Inventions*.

Which gadget

– allows you to take off your shoes without bending down?
– prevents you from feeling dizzy if your office is on the 40th floor?
– saves you from having to look a fish in the eye when you chop its head off?
– discourages people from treading on your toes when you're in the underground?
– makes it easier for you to put in your eyedrops?
– enables you to transfer chopped vegetables directly into the pan?

A

B

C

D

E

F

make it (easier)
allow
enable
prevent
stop
save
encourage
discourage

2 Look at the gadgets on page 99. What do you think they are used for, and how do they work? Talk about them using the verbs in the box.

4 Pros and cons

 Writing skills: organising information

1 Look at the text, which describes some of the advantages and disadvantages
   of living in a foreign country.

   How could you fit the sentences on the left into the text? How do you think they improve it?
   Where would you divide the text into paragraphs?

One of the most exciting things about
being abroad is that …

Another interesting thing is that …

But being in a foreign country can also
be difficult. One problem is that …

As a result …

> Everything you do is a challenge. You feel you've really
> achieved something if you manage to go across town by bus or
> buy a loaf of bread. Everything's slightly different from your
> own country – the food, the buildings, the way people dress.
> It's rather like being a child again and seeing everything for
> the first time. Even when you're having a good time, you
> remain an outsider. Even if people are really friendly, you can
> never completely become part of their world. You can easily
> feel lonely, and start missing your family or friends. That's
> when you want to go back home again.

2 Match the topics on the left below with the comments on the right.
   Expand them into sentences using the expressions in the box.

advantage of	disadvantage of	trouble with
(good) thing about	drawback of	problem with

being an only child   you don't have to do your own washing
having older brothers and sisters   you have more chance to play outside
having younger brothers and sisters   you don't have to tidy up for anyone else
living with your parents   you often have to look after them
living on your own   you meet people with all kinds of different backgrounds
growing up in a city   you don't get new clothes very often
growing up in the country   you often have no one to play with

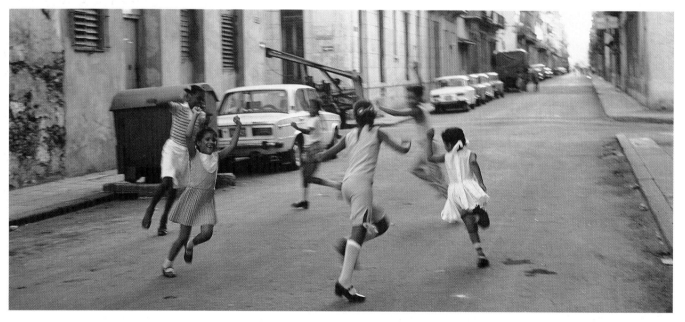

3 Look at the topics again. Which of them have you experienced yourself?
   Choose one, and find someone else who has had the same experience.

   Together make brief notes under two headings: *Good points* and *Bad points*.

   Expand your notes into two paragraphs, one describing the good points and
   the other the bad points.

Focus on Form

1 Time comparison

Here are some sentences written by a 28-year-old woman in which she says how she has changed over a period of time.

> I was much more fashion-conscious then, more ambitious, more interested in making money.
>
> I'm not nearly as well off financially as I was then.
>
> I go out in the evenings far less than I used to.
>
> I'm not as selfish as I was then. Nowadays I haven't got time to think about myself.
>
> I'm not as physically active as I used to be — I used to do lots of dangerous sports, but nowadays I'm quite happy just going for a walk.
>
> I'm a lot happier than I was, much more relaxed, and much more confident, too.

How long ago do you think she is talking about, and what do you think has happened in between?

Now think of a time when you were different from the way you are now, and write a similar set of sentences. Use this list of topics to help you.

appearance	interests	attitudes
personality	social life	food
money	fitness	knowledge
work	skills	happiness

When you've finished, show your sentences to another student. Can they guess how long ago you're talking about, and what has happened in between?

2 There's no point …

Student A: Read out each remark in Box A twice, once using *There's no point in …* or *It's not worth …*, and once using *It's not a good idea to …*

Student B: Read out a suitable continuation from Box B.

Examples:

A There's no point in / It's not worth taking a camera.
B You aren't allowed to take photos anyway.

A It's not a good idea to take a camera.
B There are a lot of thieves about.

Box A
a Let's not take the lift …
b Don't offer him a bribe …
c Let's not invite him …
d Don't take that cough mixture …

Box B
… it'll make your hair fall out.
… he's terribly boring.
… he'll probably report you to the police.
… it won't do you any good.
… he only lives on the first floor.
… he's far too honest.
… someone got stuck in it the other day.
… he's always busy on Friday nights.

---

3 Causative verbs

Make six sensible sentences from the table.

One good thing about The trouble with	having a credit card	
	being drunk	is that …
	having a large dog	

… it	forces you	from thinking clearly.
	enables you	to go for a long walk every day.
	prevents people	carrying cash around all the time.
	saves people	to forget all about your troubles.
	encourages you	from visiting you.
	discourages people	to spend more than you can afford.

Now choose an item from the box below, and make a sentence about one of its advantages or disadvantages. Can other students guess what item you're talking about?

Example: It prevents you from getting to sleep.
Answer: Drinking coffee.

doing military service	drinking coffee
having a mobile phone	not having a TV
having a burglar alarm	reading in bed
having an alarm clock	being very tall

12 Yourself and others

1 The egg test

Many countries have a tradition of painting patterns on eggs at Easter time.

Before you start the activity, choose two of the eggs below: the one you like most, and the one you like second best.

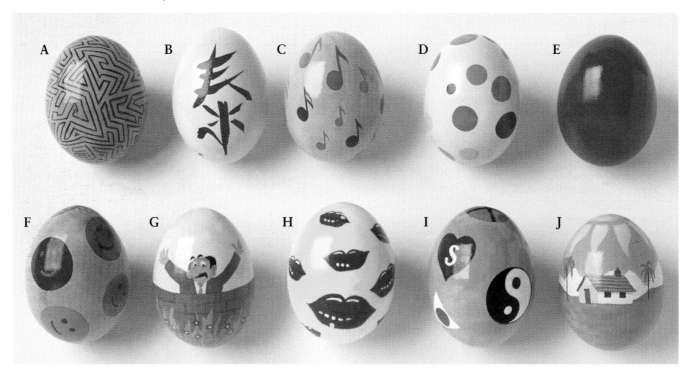

1 *a* The eggs in the picture were used as part of a personality test in a magazine.
Here are two of the interpretations. Which of the eggs do you think they go with?

Everything in its place
You're a naturally cautious person, and sometimes you tend to be a bit too precise and fussy. You always make sure you do everything thoroughly. In fact sometimes you're so afraid of making mistakes that you're not satisfied until you've cleared up every single point.

Admired by everyone
You're an active and sociable person who likes to take part in things and enjoys being the centre of attention. Although you have a tendency to be rather vain and self-centred, other people don't seem to mind, probably because you give people at least as much as you take from them.

b These sets of character adjectives go with the other eight eggs.
Which do you think go with which?

– superstitious, optimistic
– calm, reflective
– placid, easy-going
– cheerful, sociable, talkative

– sensitive, insecure
– inquisitive, nosy
– light-hearted, carefree, optimistic
– passionate, aggressive, determined

Now check your answers against the magazine's interpretations on page 100.

2 Look again at what the magazine says about the two eggs you chose.
Does it describe what you're really like?

2 Relationships

1 🔲 You will hear seven people saying what they look for in a relationship. Listen, and note down the main point each speaker makes.

What other things might be important in a relationship? Add other ideas to the list.

2 Choose three things you yourself would look for in a relationship, and write them down in order of importance.

Does anyone else have exactly the same list as you?

3 Social comment

1 Look at these cartoons, four of which have their captions missing. Which of them do you think is about
 – the relationship between wife and husband?
 – the relationship between father and son?
 – the problems of bringing up children?
 – envy between neighbours?
 – unwelcome visitors?
 – loneliness?

Which four cartoons do you think need captions? Choose one of them, and make up a caption for it.

The teacher will read out the original captions. Were they as good as yours?

A

B

C

D

2 These cartoons were all originally published in Britain.

Imagine you were making a collection of cartoons entitled *Social Comment*, for publication in your own country. Which of these cartoons would you include? Which wouldn't you include? Why?

E

F

4 Skin deep

READING

1 *Before you read*

Without looking at the article, try to guess the answers to these questions.

a Why are tattoos associated with sailors? *b* How is tattooing done? *c* How far back does tattooing go? *d* Where on the body do people have tattoos?

e Does it hurt? *f* Is it dangerous? *g* How long do tattoos last? *h* Can tattoos be removed?

Now read the article. What were the answers?

2 Look at these tattoos. Which of the styles described in the article do you think they are?

3 What problems might you have if you
   a went to a 'scratcher'?
   b took aspirin before being tattooed?
   c had a tattoo on your cheek?
   d tattooed the name of someone you're in love with?
   e had a tattoo removed?

LISTENING

You will hear an interview with a tattoo artist.

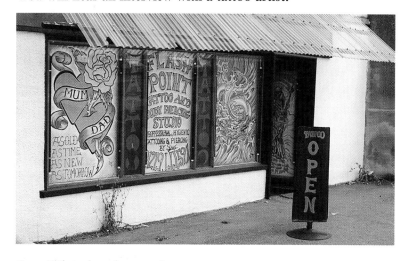

1 Imagine you were conducting the interview. What would you ask him about?

Write down two or three questions.

Now listen to the interview. Does he answer any of your questions?

2 *a* What does he say about
   – Holland? – portrait and reproduction work? – department stores?
   – scars? – tattoos on the face and hands? – the Royal Family?

b Who is Winnie and what does he look like?

3 Imagine someone gave you a voucher for a free tattoo. Would you use it? If so, what would you have done?

Skin Deep

Not so long ago, tattoos were definitely NOT the thing to do. Fashions change, however, and tattoos are fast becoming a common sight. But before you rush to join the likes of Edward VII, Janis Joplin and Sean Connery, pause for a moment – getting a tattoo is a lot easier (and cheaper) than getting rid of one.

The art of tattooing goes back a long way. The Egyptians used to tattoo each other 3,000 years ago, and the oldest known example is on the body of a 4,000 year old 'ice-man' who was found frozen in mountain snow on the Italian–Austrian border in 1993. The picture shows a tattoo on the upper arm of another ice-man, who died 2,500 years ago in Siberia, and who is now on display in a Moscow museum.

In more modern times, tattoos were reintroduced to Europe by Captain Cook and his crew on their return from Tahiti in 1771 – hence the traditional association of tattoos with sailors. The word 'tattoo' itself comes from the Tahitian word 'tatau' – onomatopoeic for the sound made by their tattooing instrument.

There are a number of major styles of tattoo, including *Tribal* (bold, simple patterns in black ink), *Celtic* (intricate knotwork, again usually black), *Oriental* (fish, clouds, dragons, etc.) and *Portrait* (images taken from photos, usually in black and grey ink). But nowadays almost any kind of image can be turned into a tattoo, in a full range of colours, and on almost any part of the body.

Technically, the only places you *can't* get tattooed are your hair, teeth and nails, but parts of the body which may change shape with ageing (such as the stomach, which tends to get bigger and sag) are best avoided. Arms and shoulders are the most popular, and one reason for this is that while these areas can be displayed in public, it is equally easy to conceal them under a shirt. For the same reason, many people choose the left wrist (which can be covered by a watch) or the feet and ankles. Some even use a shaved area of the head – and can then grow their hair to cover it up again if they want to.

Tattoos are put in place by means of a tattoo gun, which has a cluster of needles which jab in and out rapidly. The artist changes colours by dipping the tip of the gun into various colour inks as a paint artist does into a palette. Being on the receiving end of a tattoo gun is a painful process, especially for the first couple of minutes; after that, the body's natural pain-killers – endorphins – start to come into play, and the pain apparently subsides into a kind of vibrating, buzzing sensation. The use of aspirins is not recommended, as they thin the blood and can lead to bleeding.

Though not pleasant, the process is not dangerous, provided the tattoo is applied by a qualified artist in a clean and properly supervised environment. Infections can, however, result from using a 'scratcher' – someone who's bought a tattoo gun by mail order and has no idea how to use it safely. For this reason, many US states have strict safety regulations concerning tattooing, and four have banned it altogether.

The main disadvantage of tattoos is that they're permanent. It is true that they tend to blur (and possibly sag) with age – but they don't go away. So it is not a decision to be taken lightly. If you might want a job as a bank clerk in a few years' time, think twice before tattooing that fire-breathing dragon on your hand. And by all means tattoo a heart with your partner's name on your arm – provided you're sure you'll feel the same way for ever.

Tattoos can be removed, but it can be a painful process and it can leave scars. Only laser treatment can remove them completely, and this is *very* expensive. In other words, it is much easier to get a tattoo than to remove one. In a recent survey, one third of men and women questioned regretted getting tattooed. So the undecided would be well advised to stick to those temporary tattoos that you put on for the evening and remove with baby oil the next day.

E Study pages

Grammar study: pronouns and determiners

1 How many?

What's the difference between the sentences in A and those in B?

A	*All* new cars are fitted with seat-belts. *Most* flats have central heating these days. *Many* deaf people are good at lip-reading. *Very few* people live to a hundred. *Almost no* pandas survive in the wild.
B	*All (of)* these clothes need washing. *Most of* the rooms have got a private bath. *Many of* his novels are set in India. *Very few of* the audience understood Italian. *None of* his children went to university.

Here are some other quantity expressions. How could you use them to replace the phrases in italics?

hardly any   not many   quite a few   nearly all

Add a suitable quantity expression to these sentences.

a Police officers carry guns.
b Men wear earrings nowadays.
c My friends are communists.
d The shops around here open on Sunday.
e Children are vaccinated against polio.
f The students in this class are female.

2 Yourself and each other

Look at these sentences. What's the difference between *blame yourself* and *blame each other*?

a You mustn't blame yourself – it wasn't your fault.
b The two drivers blamed each other for the accident.

Fill the gaps with a verb from the box plus either *myself/yourself* etc. or *each other / one another*.

be ashamed of	help	talk to
enjoy	introduce	recognise
express		

a I believe neighbours should .... when times are bad.
b We'd like to .... I'm Bob, and this is Hilary.
c They haven't .... since they split up last year.
d Take your hands off me! You should ....
e He can understand French, but he can't .... very easily.
f Just .... to anything from the fridge.
g Now everybody, just relax and .... !
h When they met again ten years later, they hardly ....

3 I did it myself

What extra meaning is given to each of these sentences by the words in italics?

a	My sister likes detective stories, but I prefer science fiction *myself*.
b	– I'm starving. – Yes, I'm pretty hungry *myself*.
c	– Isn't that a Picasso over there? – No. I painted it *myself*.
d	Mummy didn't help me tie my shoelaces. I did them *by myself*.

Complete these sentences, using *yourself, himself*, **etc.**

a All their friends recommended the play, so they …
b Did someone give her that car, or did she …?
c Do you like our house? We …
d Some people are crazy about Volvos, but I …
e – Who helped him with his homework?
   – No one! He …

4 One and ones

A	I'd like a Coke. A large one, please. The green sweets are horrible, but I rather like the red ones.
B	I usually drink instant coffee, but I occasionally drink Turkish (coffee). I don't like white bread. I prefer brown (bread).
C	Do you want a can opener or a bottle opener? I haven't got any tennis balls, but I've got some table tennis balls.

When do we use *one* and *ones*? When can't we use *one* and *ones*?

Complete these remarks, using *one/ones* **where possible.**

a This screwdriver's too big. Have you got … ?
b Are those plastic flowers or … ?
c Italian ice-cream is much better than …
d Would you like a vanilla ice-cream or … ?
e I hate hot weather; I much prefer …
f The older children are allowed to go home for lunch, but … at school.
g That's not a carving knife – it's a …
h This exercise is boring. Can we … ?

Language awareness: regional accents

1 🔲 You will hear seven people talking about their childhood. Where do you think they come from? Match them with the places shown below.

2 🔲 You will hear the same speakers reading this extract from a novel. What features of the accent do you notice?

It was almost eight o'clock when the phone rang in the hall. I hesitated for a moment, then decided to answer it. 'Hello' said a voice. 'It's Peter. What happened to you last night?'

3 Can you think of other examples of these regional accents that you've heard before (e.g. elsewhere in this book, on television, people you've met)?

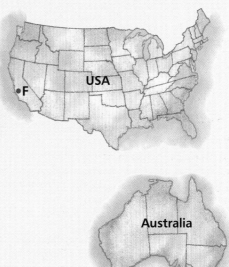

Pronunciation: low key

1 🔲 Listen to the recording, and notice how the speaker says the underlined words. Where does her voice *go down*, and where does it *go up*?

... Right, so that's the answer to Question Two. Now the third question you'll probably find a bit easier ...

2 🔲 Listen to these stretches of speech. Underline the words where the speaker's voice goes down, and where it goes up.

1 ... and that's how we eventually got to Moscow. Getting to Delhi wasn't nearly so exciting ...

2 ... I'd like to thank Dr James for coming to talk to us. Our next speaker is from the University of Oxford ...

3 ... So that was really what Freud thought about it. Now Jung's ideas about dreams were quite different ...

4 ... so we're expecting about thirty people. As for the food, that's being taken care of by my brother-in-law ...

Now try saying the remarks yourself, making 'steps up' and 'steps down' on the underlined words.

3 In writing, we can mark out extra information by using commas or brackets.

Examples:

Mr Brown, the managing director, has asked me to contact you.
I've got an elder brother (who lives in Canada) and two younger sisters.

🔲 Listen to the recording. How do we mark out extra information when we speak?

4 Which parts of these remarks do you think are 'extra information'? Put brackets round them, and then try saying each remark.

1 ... my sister who's a doctor is a neighbour of yours ...

2 ... and so I went to see Marco a friend of mine about the problem ...

3 ... her fourth book entitled 'Falling Leaves' was probably her most popular...

🔲 Now listen and see if you were right. Then practise saying the remarks again.

13 Right and wrong

1 Was justice done?

should(n't) have done /been + -ing

82-year-old man who shot burglar must pay him £4000

AN 82-YEAR-OLD MAN who shot a burglar who was trying to break into his allotment shed was ordered to pay him £4000 damages yesterday. Ted Newbery had been sleeping in the shed to try to stop vandals destroying his allotment. He fired through a hole in the door when he heard voices outside. Mark Revill, 28, was hit in the chest and arm by 50 shotgun pellets as he and another man tried to smash their way into the shed. They had gone there to steal, knowing that the pensioner had a television set and a washing machine in the shed.

Mr Newbery had slept in the shed every night for four years because of vandalism,

the court was told by the defence. That night, he heard a loud banging on the door, and a voice saying 'If the old man's in there, we'll do him.' He was absolutely terrified, and fired the gun in self-defence. As a result of the incident, Mr Revill lost two fingers, and has partially lost the use of one arm.

Mr Justice Rougier ruled that Mr Newbery had acted out of all proportion to the threat. He had not acted in panic, but had planned his response in advance, and it had been reckless to shoot the shotgun through a hole in the door, while not being able to see what he was shooting at.

Mr Justice Rougier award-

ed Revill £4000 for his injuries and loss of earnings.

The judgment caused an immediate public outcry. Tim Molloney, the Mayor of Erewash, launched an appeal to raise money to pay Mr Newbery's bill, and started the fund with a contribution of £100. Since then, money has been pouring in from all

over the country. A London restaurateur was one of the dozens to call *The Times* to express his anger over the affair. Husseyin Ozer, 42, said he would sell his Rolex watch to pay the award. 'I am outraged. The old saying that an Englishman's home is his castle does not seem to be true any more,' he said.

---

1 Read the newspaper story. Which of the opinions below do you agree with? Give each a score from 0 (= strongly disagree) to 5 (= strongly agree).

A Mr Newbery was right to try to defend himself, but he should have fired a warning shot, or shouted a warning first.

B Mr Newbery had no right to shoot Mr Revill, even in self-defence. He should have been sent to prison for what he did.

C As the police weren't protecting Mr Newbery, he had no choice but to try to protect himself.

D It was Mr Revill's own fault if he was injured – he shouldn't have been trying to break in.

E The Mayor of Erewash was quite right to start a fund to help Mr Newbery.

F The whole thing's crazy. Mr Revill should have been ordered to pay Mr Newbery £4000, not the other way around.

2 Read the article *Yes, justice was done* on page 101, and answer the questions.

Now look at the six opinions again. Have you changed you mind about any of them since reading the article?

2 Mistakes

could/needn't/should(n't) have done

1 Here is the end of a story. Choose the structures
that you think fit the meaning best.

> … Of course, as soon as I went in the room, I realised that I
> *needn't/shouldn't* have spent all that time dressing up in a dinner
> jacket. I *could/should* have just worn jeans, like everyone else.

Now look at these other two stories.
How do you think they end?

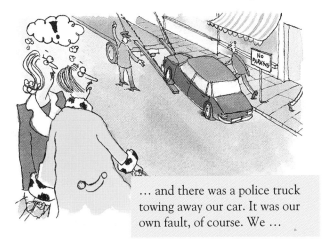

> … and there was a police truck
> towing away our car. It was our
> own fault, of course. We …

> … It was only when I
> finally staggered up to
> the ninth floor that I
> realised that 'Aufzug'
> means 'lift'. So it
> turned out that I …

2 Think of a time when something similar happened to you, and
write a sentence about it using one of the structures in the box.

Tell another student what happened.
Include your sentence in what you say.

| could have | should have |
| needn't have | shouldn't have |

3 Speaking your mind

couldn't /needn't /might have done

1 Look at each of these remarks. What can you tell about the speaker and the situation?

1 You could have told
me earlier.

2 You could have been
knocked over.

3 We might just as well
have stayed at home.

4 You might have offered
to lend a hand.

5 Huh! I might have
known!

6 You needn't have
been quite so rude.

7 You needn't have
bothered.

Now listen to the remarks in context. Were you right?

2 Think of things you might say to
 – someone who's been walking around the streets alone late at night
 – someone who's just arrived at your house three hours late
 – someone who's just slapped a child
 – someone who's forgotten your birthday
 – someone who hasn't eaten a meal you've cooked.

4 Points of view

1 Look at paragraphs A–D. What do they have in common, and how are they different? What expressions do they use to contrast the two different points of view?

Do zoos help to educate people about wildlife and the environment? Or do they encourage people to see animals as a form of entertainment?

B Unfortunately, zoos often encourage people to see animals as a form of entertainment. But they also do a lot to educate people about wildlife and the environment.

A Zoos are often accused of encouraging people to see animals as a form of entertainment. In fact, however, zoos do a lot to educate people about wildlife and the environment.

C To a certain extent it's true that zoos educate people about wildlife and the environment. On the other hand, they also encourage people to see animals as a form of entertainment.

D It isn't really true that zoos educate people about wildlife and the environment. On the contrary, they encourage people to see animals as a form of entertainment.

2 Choose one of these opinions. What arguments are there for and against it? Make some notes.

> Sending criminals to prison is a complete waste of time.

> Women and men now have equal opportunities in society.

> Doing military service makes young people into better citizens.

Develop your notes into a short paragraph (two or three sentences) that represents your own point of view. Use the expressions in Part 1 to help you.

3 Here is a longer version of paragraph C in Part 1. Notice how examples and further comments have been added to it.

> To a certain extent it's true that zoos educate people about wildlife and the environment – or at least they try to. It's common in zoos nowadays to find information about where the animals live in the wild and how they behave, or about how different animals depend on each other for survival.
>
> On the other hand, they also encourage people to see animals as a form of entertainment. You can see this in any monkey house: usually, people go there not to learn about how monkeys behave, but because they find their behaviour amusing. In fact, many species of monkey are in serious danger because of what human beings are doing to them, and this is really a reason to be angry, not to laugh.

Expand your own paragraph in a similar way.

Focus on Form

1 Forms of 'should'

Rewrite these remarks using an appropriate form of *should*.

Example:

What's he doing sitting in my chair?
Answer: *He shouldn't be sitting in my chair.*

a She had no right to take the car without asking.
b Why isn't there a name-plate on the door?
c I can't understand why you weren't wearing a crash helmet.
d It was a mistake to pull down that lovely old house.
e It seems wrong for those children to be playing in the road.
f Why wasn't this mistake noticed before?
g It's their own fault: they weren't wearing gloves, were they?

2 Needn't, couldn't & should(n't)

Look at the comic strip below. Talk about the mistakes the man made, using *needn't, couldn't, should* and *shouldn't*.

Example:

He needn't have bought his whisky and cigarettes at a supermarket. He could have got them in the duty free shop.

3 Could have & might have

Match the remarks in Box A with the most suitable continuations in Box B. Fill the gaps in the continuations with *could have, might have* or *might as well have*.

> **Box A**
>
> 1 I don't know why we bothered to see that film.
> 2 I thought you'd lost your way.
> 3 Didn't you see the red flag flying?
> 4 It wasn't really worth taking a taxi.
> 5 You shouldn't have sheltered under a tree.
> 6 That's just typical of him.
> 7 I didn't know you'd been on holiday.

> **Box B**
>
> a You .... drowned.
> b You .... been struck by lightning.
> c I .... known he'd turn up late.
> d You .... sent me a postcard.
> e You .... told me you'd be late.
> f We .... walked.
> g We .... stayed at home and watched TV.

When my uncle flew to Spain last year, he'd never been on a plane before, and he got quite a few things wrong ...

A

He went to the supermarket and bought whisky and cigarettes.

B

He got to the airport five hours before his flight took off.

C

When he got on board, he sat in the first empty seat he saw.

D

As they were taking off, he made a call on his mobile phone.

E

Then he ate the sandwiches he'd brought for the journey.

F

After lunch, he went to the toilet and had a cigarette.

G

As they were landing, he pulled down his table and started to write postcards.

H

At the airport, he paid a fortune for a taxi to the city centre.

14 Body and mind

1 Small but deadly

DANGER OF CHOLERA IN REFUGEE CAMPS, WARNS UN

Teenagers say Aids is their biggest fear

Britain to keep rabies law

Tourists warned after malaria death

1 Look at these newspaper headlines. Imagine what the articles that go with them might say. Which pictures go with which headlines? What's the connection?

2 Work in groups. Choose one of the diseases. Discuss what you know about it and what you think you know. Try to answer these questions.

   a How widespread is the disease?
   b What causes it and how is it transmitted?
   c What are the symptoms?
   d How can you avoid catching it?
   e Is it curable?

Now check your answers in the back of the book. Use a dictionary to help you.

Did you find out anything that you didn't know before? Tell the rest of the class about it.

2 Medical treatment

1 🔲 You will hear seven short scenes. Listen and say what is happening in each one. Use the words in the box.

examine	surgeon
filling	temperature
operation	thermometer
plaster	vaccination
prescribe	x-ray

2 Do any of the scenes you heard remind you of a similar experience of your own? Tell other students about it.

3 Alternative medicine

1 🔲 You will hear a story about two different methods of treating a scorpion sting. Listen and answer the questions.

a What was the 'Western' method of treatment?
b What was the traditional method of treatment?
c What was the result of each form of treatment?

What does the speaker seem to think about what he saw?

What do you think about it?
Can you think of an explanation for what happened?

2 Do you know anyone who has used any of the treatments below?
What were they treated for?

– traditional folk medicine   – hypnotherapy
– acupuncture   – faith healing
– homeopathy

Would you consider using any of these treatments as an alternative to going to the doctor? Why / Why not?

4 All the perfumes of Arabia

READING

Have you ever seen or read Shakespeare's *Macbeth*?

yes   no

What do you know about the characters in the box? How do they fit into the story?	Read the synopsis of the play on page 103.
Now check your answers on page 103.	What have you learned about the characters in the box?

Macbeth	the three witches	King Duncan	Macduff
Banquo	Lady Macbeth	Duncan's sons	

READING AND LISTENING

You will read and hear the sleepwalking scene from *Macbeth*.

PART 1: LINES 1–31

Read lines 1–31. How many of these questions can you answer?
a Where is Macbeth?
b According to the gentlewoman, what does Lady Macbeth do at night?
c Why won't the gentlewoman reveal what Lady Macbeth says?
d What is she doing with her hands?

🔲 Now listen to a modern English version of these lines. Are your answers still the same?

PART 2: LINES 32–68

Read lines 32–68. Use the notes under the text to help you understand it, but do not try to understand every word.

🔲 Now listen to the same lines being performed by Shakespearean actors, and answer the questions.
a How would you describe what's wrong with Lady Macbeth?
b During this part of the scene, Lady Macbeth relives some of the things that happened earlier in the play. Can you identify some of them? Use the synopsis to help you.

PART 3: LINES 69–80

🔲 Listen to the last lines of the scene, and follow them on the page.
What does the doctor seem to be saying, and how does he seem to feel?

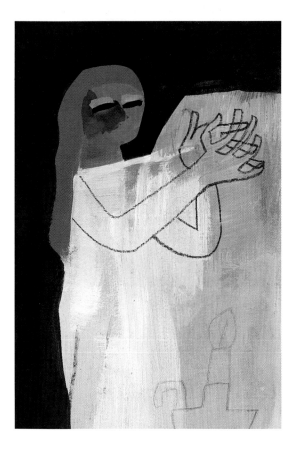

Act V Scene 1

***Enter a Doctor of Physic and a
Waiting-Gentlewoman***

DOCTOR I have two nights watched with you, but can
perceive no truth in your report. When was it she last
walked?

GENTLEWOMAN Since his majesty went into the field I
5 have seen her rise from her bed, throw her nightgown
upon her, unlock her closet, take forth paper, fold it,
write upon't, read it, afterwards seal it, and again
return to bed; yet all this while in a most fast sleep.

DOCTOR A great perturbation in nature, to receive at
10 once the benefit of sleep and do the effects of
watching. In this slumbery agitation, besides her
walking and other actual performances, what, at any
time, have you heard her say?

GENTLEWOMAN That, sir, which I will not report after
15 her.

DOCTOR You may to me; and 'tis most meet you
should.

GENTLEWOMAN Neither to you nor anyone, having no
witness to confirm my speech.

Enter Lady Macbeth with a taper

20 Lo you! Here she comes. This is her very guise; and,
upon my life, fast asleep. Observe her; stand close.

DOCTOR How came she by that light?

GENTLEWOMAN Why, it stood by her. She has light by
her continually; 'tis her command.

25 **DOCTOR** You see her eyes are open.

GENTLEWOMAN Ay, but their sense are shut.

DOCTOR What is it she does now? Look how she rubs
her hands.

GENTLEWOMAN It is an accustomed action with her to
30 seem thus washing her hands. I have known her
continue in this a quarter of an hour.

LADY Yet here's a spot.

DOCTOR Hark! She speaks. I will set down what comes
from her to satisfy my remembrance the more strongly.

35 **LADY** Out, damned spot! Out, I say! – One: two: why
then, 'tis time to do't. – Hell is murky! – Fie, my
lord, fie! A soldier and afeard? – What need we fear
who knows it, when none can call our power to
accompt? – Yet who would have thought the old man
40 to have had so much blood in him?

DOCTOR Do you mark that?

LADY The Thane of Fife had a wife; where is she now?
– What, will these hands ne'er be clean? – No more
o'that, my lord, no more o'that. You mar all with this
starting.　　　　　　　　　　　　　　　　　　　　　　　45

DOCTOR Go to, go to: you have known what you should
not.

GENTLEWOMAN She has spoke what she should not, I
am sure of that. Heaven knows what she has known.

LADY Here's the smell of the blood still. All the　　　50
perfumes of Arabia will not sweeten this little hand.
Oh! Oh! Oh!

DOCTOR What a sigh is there! The heart is sorely
charged.

GENTLEWOMAN I would not have such a heart in my　55
bosom for the dignity of the whole body.

DOCTOR Well, well, well.

GENTLEWOMAN Pray God it be, sir.

DOCTOR This disease is beyond my practice; yet I have
known those which have walked in their sleep who　60
have died holily in their beds.

LADY Wash your hands; put on your nightgown; look
not so pale. I tell you yet again, Banquo's buried; he
cannot come out on's grave.

DOCTOR Even so?　　　　　　　　　　　　　　　　　65

LADY To bed, to bed! There's knocking at the gate.
Come, come, come, come, give me your hand. What's
done cannot be undone. To bed, to bed, to bed.

Exit

DOCTOR Will she go now to bed?

GENTLEWOMAN Directly.　　　　　　　　　　　　　70

DOCTOR Foul whisperings are abroad, unnatural deeds
Do breed unnatural troubles; infected minds
To their deaf pillows will discharge their secrets.
More needs she the divine than the physician.
God, God forgive us all! Look after her,　　　　　75
Remove from her the means of all annoyance
And still keep eyes upon her. So, good night.
My mind she has mated, and amazed my sight.
I think, but dare not speak.

GENTLEWOMAN Good night, good doctor.　　　　　80

Notes on lines 32–68

33 *set down* write down
34 *satisfy my remembrance* support
my memory
36 *murky* dark
36 *Fie!* Shame on you!
37 *afeard* afraid

38 *call our power to accompt*
challenge our power
44 *mar all* spoil everything
45 *starting* jumping with fright
53 *sorely charged* badly troubled
59 *beyond my practice* outside my
experience

Notes on lines 69–80

73 *discharge* tell
74 *divine* priest
76 *means of all annoyance*
anything that might be dangerous
78 *mated* confused

Study pages

Grammar study: degree and comparison

1 Too and enough

too	too much	too many	enough

Add an item from the box to each of these sentences, so that they make sense.

a There weren't chairs for everyone to sit down.
b Are you old to vote?
c I'm tired to go out tonight.
d I think I've had to eat.
e She didn't run fast to catch the bus.
f Don't eat sweets or you'll be ill.
g There's just coffee for three cups.
h He took the bend quickly and skidded off the road.
i You smoke.

2 So and such

Look at these examples. **When do we use *so* and when do we use *such*?**

A	This coffee's so strong that I can't drink it. She drove so fast that I was terrified.
B	It was such a boring speech that I fell asleep. It was such lovely weather that we ate outside.
C	I've got so much luggage that I can't carry it all. So few people came that we cancelled the meeting.

Add *so* or *such* or *such a(n)* to the following:

cold	much food	good time
cold weather	bad food	many times
noisy	little food	intelligent
noisy party	slowly	bad temper

Choose three of the items and include them in sentences of your own.

3 Two kinds of adjective

What is the difference between the adjectives in Box A and those in Box B? What else could we say instead of *very* and *absolutely*?

A		B	
(very)	tired clever hungry upset nasty hot	(absolutely)	exhausted brilliant ravenous heart-broken revolting boiling

Which group do these adjectives belong to, A or B? Can you think of their equivalent in the other group?

angry	enormous	pleased
cold	filthy	spotless
deafening	hilarious	surprised

Student A: Ask a question using a type A adjective.
Student B: Respond using a type B adjective.

Example: A Was he upset when she left?
　　　　　　 B Yes. He was absolutely heart-broken.

4 Comparison

Each of these sentences contains a mistake. Can you correct them?

a She's much more taller than her brother.
b Goats aren't as stupid than sheep.
c He writes far tidier than I do.
d I'm heavier than him ten kilos.
e He's most boring person I've ever met.
f Everest is the most high mountain in the world.
g The United States isn't nearly bigger than Canada.
h It wasn't as interesting as I expected it.

5 Numerical comparison

T-shirts $15	sweatshirts $30	jumpers $45

Sweatshirts are twice as expensive as the price of T-shirts.

Jumpers are three times as expensive as the price of T-shirts.

How would these comparisons change

a if T-shirts only cost $14?
b if T-shirts cost $16?
c if you couldn't remember the exact prices?

Complete the table, then complete the comparison beside each item. If you don't know the answer, make a guess.

Adjective	Noun	
long	length	a The Suez Canal .... the Panama Canal.
high		b Mount Everest .... Mount Fuji.
heavy		c A fully grown elephant .... a baby elephant.
old		d The Great Pyramid .... the Great Wall of China.
big		e The Pacific Ocean .... the Indian Ocean.

Language awareness: formal and informal

1 Here are some examples of formal English. Where would you expect to see or hear them?

   a We regret that we are unable to offer you any further assistance in this matter.
   b I was proceeding along the High Street when I observed two men attempting to force an entry into a parked car.
   c The dining car is situated towards the rear of the train.
   d The consumption of alcoholic beverages on the premises is strictly forbidden.
   e I would like to express my sincere appreciation of the fact that such a large number people have attended this meeting.

   Imagine you're passing on these pieces of information to someone else. How would you express them in a more informal style?

   Now listen to the recording. How similar were your answers to the ones you heard?

2 Notice that we tend to use phrasal verbs in informal English. Here are some sentences with phrasal verbs. Match them with the more formal verbs in the box.

recover	ascertain	respect	tolerate
consider	investigate	postpone	

   a I'll have to *think* it *over*.
   b They *put off* the meeting till the next day.
   c I can't *put up with* it any longer.
   d It took her a long time to *get over* it.
   e I'll *look into* it next week.
   f We need to *find out* exactly what happened.
   g I've always *looked up to* him.

3 Abstract nouns are often used in formal English. Can you identify the abstract nouns in these sentences? Rewrite them to make them less formal.

   a There's a severe shortage of qualified teachers in this area.
   b There are plenty of good restaurants in the vicinity of Times Square.
   c You are under no obligation to buy it.
   d Do you have any objection to my smoking?
   e He has a tendency to use formal English.

Pronunciation: disagreeing politely

1 You will hear this conversation twice. What is the difference between the two replies? Which reply sounds more polite? Why?

   A I hear you lost again on Saturday.
   B No, we won.

2 You will hear the questions below, with the replies said in two different ways. Which replies sound polite? How do the others sound?

   1 A I don't suppose she'll pass, will she?
      B Yes. I think she's got a good chance.
   2 A You'll be going to Italy again, won't you?
      B No, we're going to Spain this year.
   3 A You don't eat meat, then?
      B I do. I'm just not hungry.

   Now listen to the conversations again, and try replying yourself in the same way.

3 Listen to these two conversations. Where does B's voice rise, and where does it fall?

   1 A Teaching must be really hard work.
      B Well yes, it can be difficult.
   2 A Teaching must be really hard work.
      B Well, it can be difficult, but I really enjoy it.

4 How do you think B's replies will sound in these conversations? Mark places where you think the voice will rise, and where it will fall.

   1 A John never seems to be here on time.
      B He's sometimes late, but he often works at the weekend, too.
   2 A Didn't you like the play?
      B I enjoyed the first half, but not the second.
   3 A You've got a house in Manchester, haven't you?
      B I used to live there, but now I've moved to London.
   4 A I like your new car.
      B It looks good, but it doesn't go very well.

   Now listen and see if you were right. Then practise saying the conversations.

15

Using the passive

1 Memories

1 You will hear three people talking about their family memories.

   a Listen to the first two and follow what they say on the page.

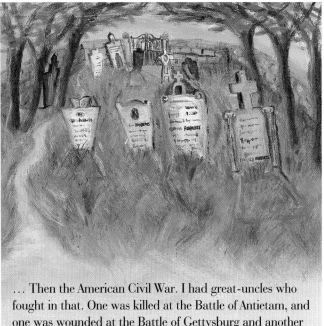

… Then the American Civil War. I had great-uncles who fought in that. One was killed at the Battle of Antietam, and one was wounded at the Battle of Gettysburg and another was killed at another battle somewhere. And they're all buried in the Roberts cemetery …

… I was the youngest of all these children in the family. And I was very well looked after, very spoiled by them. I could play in all their games. I was never left out. All the rest of them used to get into trouble. I never got into trouble. They used to get spanked. I never used to get spanked. So I used to, not enjoy it, but I used to get away with a lot of things …

Find examples of the passive in each extract.
Why do the speakers choose to use the passive?

   b Here is what the third speaker says, but all the verbs have been put into the active.
Where do you think the speaker might use the passive?

When I was 13, they sent my parents abroad.
My parents didn't want to disrupt my education.
They sent me to a boarding school.
I really hated it.
We had to go to bed at 9.30.
They didn't allow us to go out in the evenings.
And of course we did all use to sneak out in the evenings.
One night they caught me.
I thought they were going to expel me.
The headmistress just wrote a letter to my parents.

 Now listen to the recording.

2 Think of a family memory of your own, and write one sentence using the passive.

   Tell another student about what happened. Include your sentence in what you say.

2 Facts and theories

Passive reporting verbs

1 These sentences from newspapers and magazines are all in rather formal English. How could you say the same things in conversational English?

> Aspirins are known to help prevent heart disease.

> The attack is believed to have been carried out by a separatist group.

> Queen Elizabeth I is said to have had a bath every month 'whether she needed it or not'.

> The royal couple are thought to be spending their honeymoon somewhere in the Caribbean.

2 Look at the sentences in the table. Are they facts or just theories? Choose the most appropriate reporting verb.

Cigarettes are	said	to cause cancer.
Lord Lucan is	believed	to have taken a ferry to France.
Dinosaurs are	known	to have been wiped out by an asteroid.

Work in groups. Choose two or three of these topics, and try to reach agreement about what is known or believed about them. Write sentences like those in the table which summarise your conclusions.

– the Yeti
– the death of Adolf Hitler
– the origins of the Aids virus
– Atlantis
– Is the sea level rising or falling?
– How did the universe begin?

Now read out your conclusions. Do other students agree with them?

3 Experiences

'have' passive

> She had her flat redecorated last week.

> I've never had my eyes tested.

> She had her driving licence taken away last week.

> I've never had my car vandalised.

> Have you ever had anything published?

> Have you ever had your fingerprints taken?

1 What do the six remarks have in common?
What's the difference between the ones on the left and the ones on the right?

2 Complete the table.

		Yes	No
Have you ever	had your fortune told?		
	had your car or bike stolen?		
	had your bag snatched?		
	had your picture printed in the paper?		
	had your face slapped?		

Work in groups. If you answered 'Yes' to any of the questions, tell the others what happened.

Now choose the most interesting experience in your group and tell the rest of the class about it.

4 One thing leads to another

1 These paragraphs all contain expressions for talking about causes and results.
Write them down in two lists: expressions used for describing *causes* or *origins*
(e.g. *was caused by*) and expressions used for describing *results* (e.g. *led to*).

The Black Death, which swept through Europe in the
14th century, resulted in more than 3 million deaths.
The plague is believed to have been caused by a virus
which originated in Central Asia and may have been
brought to Europe by Genghis Khan's invading armies.

The economic recession in the late 1980s
caused a sharp drop in house prices. As a result,
many people who would otherwise have sold
their houses decided not to move. This led to a
period of stagnation in the housing market,
which kept house prices low for several years.

Fax and email have made it possible to communicate much faster and more effectively over long
distances. One result of this has been that more
people are now able to work from home instead of
travelling to work.

The exact cause of the strike is still unclear, but it is
thought to have been due to dissatisfaction about pay
offered to part-time workers.

2 Here are three paragraphs about global warming, which all express the same idea. What
is the difference between them? What other expressions could you use instead of the
phrases in italics?

a Global warming has already *led to* noticeable changes in the world's climate.

b Over the past two decades, the temperature of the Earth's atmosphere has gradually
increased. *As a result*, the world's climate has become less stable: some areas have
experienced unusually high temperatures and droughts, while other areas have suffered
from heavy rainfall and violent storms.

c Over the last two decades, the world's climate has become less stable: some areas have
experienced unusually high temperatures and droughts, while other areas have suffered
from heavy rainfall and violent storms. Scientists believe that these changes *are* at least
partly *caused by* global warming.

3 Choose one of these headlines, and expand the ideas into a paragraph, using the
expressions you have noted down. Put the ideas together in any order you like, and add
any ideas of your own. Then compare paragraphs with other students.

A
EXPLOSION KILLS 20 PEOPLE

(leaking gas pipe – damaged when road was
repaired – explosion – 20 people killed)

D
More illiterate children, warns report

(cuts in education – fewer teachers –
more children unable to read or write)

B
INNER CITY VIOLENCE:
'We're moving out,' say residents

(increase in crime in inner city areas –
people moving to suburbs – cities will
become even more dangerous)

C
Arctic weather brings chaos to roads

(heavy snow and high winds – chaos on
roads – cars abandoned – electricity cut off)

Focus on Form

1 Forms of the passive

Rewrite these sentences using the passive.

a They hold elections every four years.
b Customs officials seized ten kilos of cocaine.
c We are considering your application.
d I discovered that someone was bugging my phone.
e Someone has already thought of that idea.
f They gave him a gold watch as a retirement present.
g Let's wait – someone might offer us a lift.
h Do we have to pay for the seats in advance?
i They should never have allowed the plan to go ahead.
j She doesn't mind people asking her awkward questions.
k I'm not used to people staring at me.

2 The passive with 'get'

Complete the remarks below with a 'get' passive, using an appropriate verb.

Example:

Some people are terrified of lifts. They think they're going to *get stuck*.

a You'd better lock your bike up. It might …
b Keep away from that wasps' nest, or …
c The last person they caught taking drugs on the school premises …
d If you walk around alone late at night, you're very likely …
e He had a very tough childhood. He used to …
f I never received your letter. It must have …

3 Passive reporting verbs

80 killed in oil explosion

An oil depot in the remote mountain town of Tigrit exploded late last night, starting a fire which spread through a southern suburb of the city. At least 80 people are known to have been killed.

Here are some statements people made about the explosion. Change them into sentences that the reporter might include in the newspaper article, using the structures in the box.

is are	known said believed thought reported understood	to …

We know that at least 80 people were killed, and they say that many more have lost their homes.

According to reports, thousands of families are camping in makeshift tents.

We believe the drinking water is contaminated by leaking oil.

The Prime Minister is visiting the area today, or so we understand.

We know that terrorist groups have been threatening to blow up the oil depot, but we think the explosion was caused accidentally.

4 The 'have' passive

Use the verbs in the box to talk about what's happening in the pictures.

Now complete the story, using the 'have' passive.

break	pick
break into	slash
cut	snatch
dump	

My neighbours Jack and Sylvia are starting to believe that someone doesn't like them very much. Last Sunday, they had their car tyres slashed. Then on Monday, …

Sunday   Monday   Tuesday

Wednesday   Thursday   Friday   Saturday

16

World affairs

1 War and peace

Rwanda, 1995

Vietnam, 1968

towns • air bases • Vietcong • damage •
forces • launch • inflict • attack

Tanzania • border • massacre •
refugees • camps • close • flee

Bosnia, 1995

presidents • peace treaty • agreement • war •
negotiations • reach • sign • end

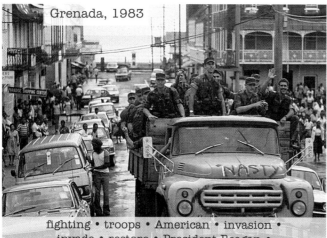

Grenada, 1983

fighting • troops • American • invasion •
invade • restore • President Reagan •
democracy • resist • protect

Chechnya, 1996

Chechen fighters • town • hostages • hospital •
tanks • spokesman • surround • warn • harm

1   The photos show scenes from five different conflicts. They were all used to accompany news reports at the time.

   Look at the words under each photo. Can you work out roughly what each story was?

   📼 Now listen to the news broadcasts. How similar were they to what you imagined?

2   Look at these quotations, which are all about war and peace.
    What point does each of them make?

> *"Peace (n.) In international affairs, a period of cheating between two periods of fighting"*
> AMBROSE BIERCE, 1906

> *"There never was a good war or a bad peace"*
> BENJAMIN FRANKLIN, 1783

> *"Patriots always talk of dying for their country, and never of killing for their country"*
> BERTRAND RUSSELL, 1938

> *"War can only be abolished through war"*
> MAO ZEDONG, 1938

> *"They make a desert and they call it peace"*
> TACITUS, 100 AD

   Make up a 'quotation' of your own about war and peace.

2 Talking politics

1 How politically aware are you? Answer the questions.

The teacher will tell you how to mark your answers. How well did you do?

---

1 About your country
  a Can you name
    – the Minister of Foreign Affairs?
    – two other members of the Cabinet?
    – the last three Prime Ministers or
      Presidents?
  b Do you know
    – how often general elections are held?
    – the year of the last general election?

2 Recent events
  Give an example of
  – a recent foreign visit by a head of state
  – a recent political scandal
  – a recent change of government

3 Something in common
  Find pairs in the box. What connects them?

Elizabeth II	Slovenia	Josef Stalin
Mozambique	Emil Zapata	Angola
Abraham Lincoln	Anwar Sadat	Estonia
Che Guevara	Benito Mussolini	Juan Carlos

4 Famous politicians
  Give three facts about each of these people.

---

2 Write one or two questions of your own, and find someone who can answer them.

3 Election issues

1 Look at these election promises. Which issue is each one about?

A We will use public money to finance a much-needed building programme in our inner cities.

B We will find sensible alternatives to sending offenders to prison.

C We will not allow foreigners to take jobs that citizens of this country could do just as well.

D We will tax pollution – the more pollution a company causes, the more it will pay.

D We believe that reducing income tax will encourage people to work hard and take more responsibility for running their own lives.

> Health
> Education
> Defence
> The economy
> Law and order
> Employment
> Housing
> Transport
> The environment
> ....
> ....
> ....

Think of the political parties in your country. Which of them do you think might make each promise?

2 Imagine a general election in your own country. What other election issues would there be? Add to the list.

Choose the three issues that you think are most important. Write two sentences about each, saying what the problem is and what should be done about it.

Now show your sentences to another student.
Can he/she guess what party you would vote for?

---

4 On the front line

READING

1 Before you read the article *Images of War*, check that you understand these words, which are all connected with war. Then read the article.

devastation	guerrillas	conflict	amputate
come under fire	ambush	mine (n.)	siege

2 How do you think David Pratt would answer these questions?

a What do you like most about being a war photographer?
b Do you think what you do changes people's attitudes?
c Do you get emotionally involved in what you see?
d Does your job interfere with your personal life?
e What do you see as the main purpose of your job?
f Do you think you're a 'war junkie'?

3 According to the article, what did David Pratt do in these places?

Afghanistan   Nicaragua   Cambodia   the West Bank   Yugoslavia

4 The article contains these idiomatic expressions. Can you guess what they mean?

a Pratt admits to '*getting a buzz*' out of taking risks.
b 'I just lay on my bed and *cried my heart out*.'
c 'It may seem *corny*, but I just try to show it the way it is.'
d 'War photography has become my life. It's what *makes me tick*.'

LISTENING

You will hear an interview with Gaby Rado, a television war correspondent.

1 Before you listen, look at these statements about his job. Which do you think are true and which are false?

a Being a war correspondent is not as dangerous as people imagine.
b The most dangerous incidents usually happen accidentally.
c He gets so involved with what he sees that it interferes with his work.
d What he sees often makes him feel angry.
e It's difficult to come back from a war zone to the 'normal' world.
f It's more difficult to be a war correspondent if you have a family.

Now listen and check your answers.

2 He tells two stories about his experiences. Here are elements from the two stories. Which belong to which story, and how do they fit together?

the front line	dead bodies	no man's land	a baby
refugees	a young woman	a village	

DISCUSSION

Both the article and the recording focus on these aspects of reporting a war:

– the risks involved in the job
– coming back to the 'real' world
– how emotionally involved the reporters get
– the effect of the job on personal relationships

How similar are the two men's experiences? What are the differences?

Images of war

What does Glaswegian David Pratt get out of being a war photographer? **Ron Farn** *explains.*

The road leading to the Pul-e-Mahmoud Khan bridge over the Kabul river was now a scene of devastation, with every building smashed beyond repair. Once at the heart of the Afghan capital, the road was almost deserted as we made our way toward the bridge which marked the front line. Suddenly a tank shell came in, followed by the rattle of automatic fire, bullets hissing past a little too close for comfort. This was far enough for me. I had all the information I needed, but David Pratt continued over the bridge to get as close as possible to the fighting, because that's what war photographers do. Why should somebody like Pratt, who studied painting and sculpture at Glasgow School of Art and later taught there, choose to go to war for a living?

"I liked the immediacy of photography," explains Pratt, "and taking photographs in a war zone is about as immediate as it gets." Pratt's first experience of war was in central America where, he told me, he froze the first time he came under fire when travelling in a column with Nicaraguan Sandinista guerrillas which drove into a Contra ambush. "That was the point when I had to decide whether I really wanted to do war photography," he says. "There is no point whatever in putting yourself in life-threatening situations if you can't take pictures. That would be insane."

Some photographers are drawn by danger and excitement, others by the idea that their pictures can bring about change. Pratt admits to "getting a buzz" out of taking risks, but argues that pictures can and do make a difference. "The images of Vietnam, particularly those of wounded US soldiers, went a long way to changing public opinion in the States. Photographs of suffering do alert public opinion, even if they don't often change the minds of politicians." Photography is by its nature an intrusive medium: the photographer is a participant rather than just an observer. This is especially true in conflicts where people's homes and families are being destroyed. In a Red Cross hospital in Cambodia, Pratt photographed victims of land mines only a few hundred yards from Khmer Rouge positions. In the fly-infested ward, doctors were amputating limbs with no anaesthetic. One Australian photographer couldn't stand it any more and left the room. Pratt stayed and shot pictures. "These situations do affect you, of course they do, but I felt I had to finish the job," he says. "Then I went back to my room in the Monorom Hotel in Phnom Penh, and I just lay on my bed and cried my heart out."

Apart from witnessing deeply disturbing events, the war correspondent often has a personal price to pay. Not only does he or she take the risks associated with the job, but there can also be tremendous pressure placed on personal relationships. It can be even harder for those left at home. Back in Pakistan, we picked up mail from home: birthday cards for me but, in Pratt's case, an altogether more serious letter.

His long-term girlfriend had had enough of worrying and waiting and had left him. I had never seen him so shaken. Returning to Glasgow, he realised there was nothing he could do, short of giving up photographing wars, but this was too high a price to pay. He threw himself into his work, travelling to the Israeli occupied West Bank and Gaza strip to report on the Intifada. In the former Yugoslavia, he crossed the lines from the Serb to the Croat side and was at the siege of Vukovar. He travelled across the killing fields of Cambodia by bus, and covered the fighting between the government forces and the Khmer Rouge.

How does Pratt reconcile his obvious concern for the victims of war with the fact that he makes his living photographing them? "With difficulty sometimes, but I have never tried to glorify war. It may sound corny, but I just try to show it the way it is, as sympathetically and compassionately as possible." It is easy to accuse photographers like Pratt of being war junkies, and he admits he would be devastated if forced to stay safely at home in Glasgow, running a photo agency. "War photography has become my life. It's what makes me tick."

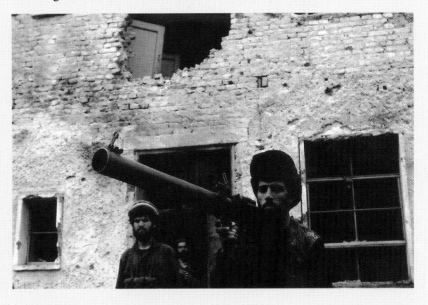

Review: Units 9–16

Find out

1 Ask other students about an argument or disagreement they've had recently.

Do you think they were in the right or in the wrong?

2 *Why do relationships break down?*

Get opinions from other students. Tell the class the results of your survey.

3 Ask one or two people what their star signs are, and what kind of character they are supposed to have.

Do they believe they really are like that?

4 Answer these questions. Say why / why not.

 – Is it worthwhile voting?
 – Do you think you will be happier in five years' time than you are now?
 – Would you like to be a war correspondent?

Compare answers with other students.

Words

1 What's the similarity between these pairs? What's the difference?

mugging	vandalism
police	vigilantes
astronomy	astrology
global warming	the hole in the ozone layer
acupuncture	hypnotherapy
refugees	casualties

2 Add words to these lists.

 – geology, physics ...
 – health, education, law and order ...

3 Give an example of

 – a revolutionary – an assassination
 – a peace treaty – an invasion
 – a massacre – a scandal

Role-play

1 A You're visiting a tropical country for the first time, and you're worried about the risks to your health.

 B Reassure your friend, and give him/her some useful advice.

2 Work in threes. Choose one of these topics and act out a short radio or TV discussion.

 Darwin got it right
 Alternative medicine works
 It's possible to foretell the future

 A You agree.
 B You disagree.
 C You're in the chair.

3 Prepare a short conversation which contains one of the following remarks.

 – You might have told me
 – You needn't have bothered
 – It was a complete waste of time
 – You had no right to ...

Writing

1 Work in groups. How much do you know about what's in today's news?

Share your information and together write a short news broadcast.

2 A You're thinking of visiting B's country for a holiday. Write to him/her, saying what you're interested in, and asking advice about where to go and what to do.

 B Write back to A, giving him/her advice about different possibilities.

3 *Giving money to help famine victims just leads to worse problems later on.*

Do you agree with this statement? Write a paragraph giving your opinion.

Talking points

Prepare a short talk (about one minute) using
one of these pictures as a starting point.

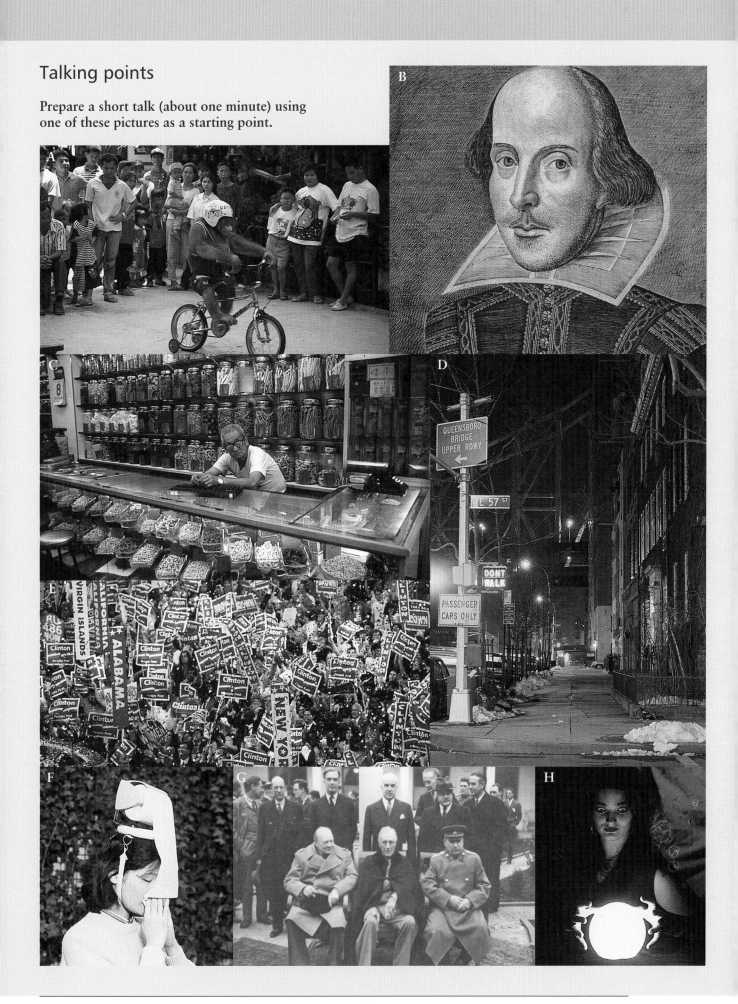

Additional material

Just the job

Flat 3
34 Marlborough Road
Birmingham

Global Travel Ltd
110 Edward Street
Birmingham

Dear Sir/Madam,

I have seen your advertisement in the *Evening News*, and I would like to apply to work in your travel agency this summer.

I have some experience of secretarial and office work. After leaving school, I worked for a firm of accountants, where I was given secretarial training and learned how to type and use a computer. I have also worked as an assistant in a department store, so I am used to dealing with customers and helping with problems.

I have visited Spain and Portugal several times, and know many of the main tourist areas in both countries. I speak Spanish fluently, and I have a basic knowledge of Portuguese. I have always been interested in travel and I have a good sense of geography.

I am an outgoing and confident person, and I think I would enjoy working for you.

I am looking forward to hearing from you.

Yours faithfully,

Diana Jarvis

Diana Jarvis

3.4 In the frame *Student A*

Joseph's Dream, by Paula Rego

Write a description of the painting. Include enough details so that someone else could visualise it.

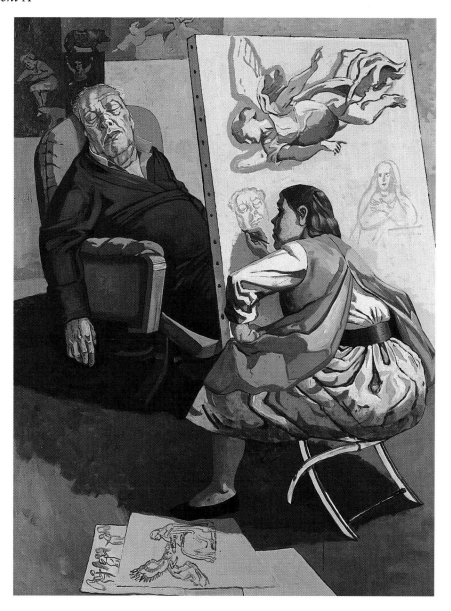

3 Focus on Form Cleft sentences with 'It' *Student A*

Which do you think are the correct choices? Check your answers with B.

Use this text to check B's answers.

Christopher Columbus

Christopher Columbus was born in *Spain/Portugal/Italy* in 1451. He believed that he could reach *India/China/ America* by sailing west. *Manuel I of Portugal / Ferdinand of Spain / Henry VII of England* eventually agreed to pay for a voyage, and in August *1492 / 1494 / 1496* he set sail on the *Santa María / Hispaniola / Mayflower* and two other ships. They reached *the coast of Labrador / the West Indies / New England* on October 12, and took the news back to Europe. After three more voyages to America, Columbus died in poverty in *Spain/Italy/Portugal* in 1506.

Marco Polo

Marco Polo grew up in Venice. In 1271 his father and uncle left on a trading expedition to China, and took Marco Polo with them, although he was only 15 years old. After travelling on horseback for several months, they eventually reached their destination, and they were invited to stay at the court of the Emperor Kublai Khan. Marco Polo entered the Emperor's service and learned to speak fluent Mongolian. He returned home 23 years later, and wrote an account of his travels.

Snare,
by Paula Rego

Write a description of the painting. Include enough details so that someone else could visualise it.

3 Focus on Form Cleft sentences with 'It' *Student B*

Use this text to check A's answers.

Which do you think are the correct choices? Check your answers with A.

Christopher Columbus

Christopher Columbus was born in Italy in 1451. He believed that he could reach India by sailing west. Ferdinand of Spain eventually agreed to pay for a voyage, and in August 1492 he set sail on the *Santa María* and two other ships. They reached the West Indies on October 12, and took the news back to Europe. After three more voyages to America, Columbus died in poverty in Spain in 1506.

Marco Polo

Marco Polo grew up in *Venice/Barcelona/Naples*. In *1271 / 1371 / 1471* his father and uncle left on a trading expedition to *India/Persia/China*, and took Marco Polo with them, although he was only 15 years old. After travelling *on foot / by ship / on horseback* for several months, they eventually reached their destination, and they were invited to stay at the court of the Emperor *Genghis Khan / Kublai Khan / Aga Khan*. Marco Polo entered the Emperor's service and learned to speak fluent *Chinese/Persian/Mongolian*. He returned home *three/23/ 43* years later, and wrote an account of his travels.

'Own goal' defender shot dead outside restaurant

A COLOMBIAN footballer was shot dead yesterday by angry fans who blamed him for their side's early exit from the World Cup. Andrés Escobar, a defender who scored an own goal during his side's defeat by the United States team, was confronted by a group of men as he left a restaurant in Medellín, 200 kilometres from Bogotá. After an argument about his poor performance, they fired 12 bullets. One of the gunmen is reported to have said to Escobar before the shooting 'Thank you for the own goal.'

Tennis stars strike it rich on and off the court

There's lots of money in tennis these days – and for the big players, a large proportion of it comes from big business.

Andre Agassi recently signed a contract with Nike worth a reputed $100 million over ten years, in addition to an estimated $8 million in prize money, and Pete Sampras this year became a Wimbledon millionaire by beating Boris Becker. Steffi Graf is generally thought to be worth more than $30 million through winnings and advertising, and Martina Navratilova, nine-time Wimbledon singles champion, has a personal fortune estimated at more than $20 million.

FOOTBALLER FACES SUSPENSION AFTER ATTACK ON SPECTATOR

ERIC CANTONA, the Manchester United striker, will probably be suspended for the rest of the season after he attacked a spectator during the match against Crystal Palace at Selhurst Park last night.

The incident happened moments after Cantona had been sent off for kicking out at another player, his sixth sending off in 16 months.

As he walked off the field, a spectator was seen running down a gangway from some 20 rows back, apparently to shout abuse at Cantona, who suddenly turned, jumped over the wall and kicked out at the man, and then punched him.

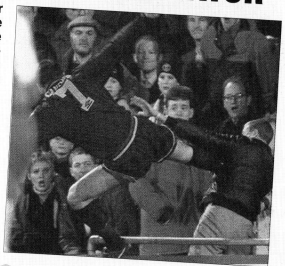

World champion swimmer suspended after drugs test

THE CHINESE WORLD CHAMPION, Lu Bin, has been suspended from all competition for two years after a positive drugs test, the International Swimming Federation announced yesterday. Lu returned a positive result for the anabolic steroid, dehydrotestosterone, in a test on September 30, shortly before the Asian Games.

Lu won four gold and two silver medals at the Games and set a world record for the 200 metres individual medley. At the world championships in Rome last September, she won the 200 metres individual medley title plus two relay gold medals.

4.4 Problems, problems …

Here are the clues for Problems 2–8.

Remember that if you look at a clue, you can only score one point for a correct answer.

Problem
2 Two boyfriends

Let's say that the trains in Bill's direction leave at 9.00, 9.10, 9.20, and so on.

To find the answer, you just have to decide when the trains leave in Mario's direction.

Supposing, for example, that they leave at 9.05, 9.15, and so on. That way, Annie would end up going to Bill half the time and Mario half the time. So that can't be right.

So when do the trains leave in Mario's direction?

Problem
3 An explosive mixture

The problem boxes are D and E – they each touch six other boxes. If 1 goes in D, what goes in E?

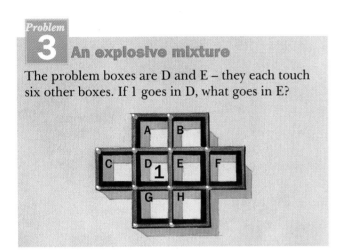

Problem
4 Sweet revenge

There are other things you can do when you move a jar, besides just picking it up and putting it down. What?

Problem
5 One man and his dog

Well, the farmer's going to walk 20 km. So how long will the dog run in the same time?

Problem
6 On balance

Try dividing the boxes into three groups of three.

Problem
7 Whodunnit?

Compare what A and B say. Then think about it.

Problem
8 Wrong labels

Try putting your hand in the bag marked 'mixed'.

Life elsewhere?

Douglas Keyworth looks at the evidence for alien forms of life

As we all know, the Earth has everything that is needed for life to develop, which is why we are here.

But four billion years ago, when the Earth was formed, what were the chances that life would emerge? Pretty small, according to biologists – about the same chance that you would have of winning the national lottery five weeks in a row. So we're quite lucky to be here at all.

Elsewhere in the Universe

What about the chances of life forming elsewhere – in our own galaxy, for instance? The Milky Way contains around 400 billion stars. Some (maybe most) of these have planets orbiting around them, and the chances are that many millions – or even billions – of these planets could support life. So it does seem possible that there are some other lottery winners living in the same neighbourhood.

And if you think that there are countless other galaxies out there – many of them far bigger than the Milky Way – then it seems obvious that there must be other forms of life somewhere in the Universe.

Intelligent life

But is it intelligent life, the kind of life that could build space ships and pay us a visit?

Here on Earth there have been billions of species, but only one of them has turned out to be intelligent enough to develop technology and fly into space. And even we're not particularly intelligent: the human race will probably blow itself up long before it learns how to visit other parts of the galaxy.

Alien visits

But let's suppose that there are advanced civilisations, here in our own galaxy, who have developed fast-moving flying saucers. Would they visit the Earth?

First we need to ask: why should they want to? The most likely answer is that their own sun is at the end of its life, and they need to find somewhere else to live.

And the next question is: why here? The diagram shows the part of the Milky Way which probably has the largest number of habitable planets. The oldest ones (and therefore the ones which are most likely to have advanced forms of life) are in the area shaded red. We're towards the edge (marked X).

|← 20,000 →|
light years

If I were an alien looking for a new home, I think I would try a few million of my neighbouring planets before bothering to travel a hundred thousand trillion miles to visit Earth, on a journey that would take at least 200,000 years.

UFOs

But what about all those UFO sightings that are reported every year? Well, most of them are planes. And whatever the others are, they're not flying saucers. If you were a visiting alien with incredibly powerful technology, what would you do: hide yourself away and keep quiet, or land and take over the Earth? I know what my answer would be.

If there are other forms of life elsewhere in the Universe (and I'm sure there are), that's exactly where they are – elsewhere.

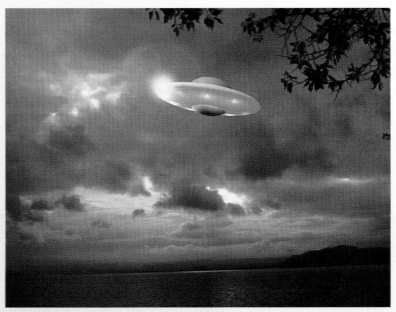

A visiting alien, a trick of the light or a fake?

© 1994 Gabriella Roth

Use these questions to help you talk about the painting.

1 Is there any relationship between the people? If so, what do you think it is?
2 Why is the woman putting her finger to her lips?
3 What are the two men doing?
4 What do you notice about these things?

   – the plant
   – the humming bird
   – the doorway
   – the old woman
   – the dog

5 The painting is called *Sirens Rising*.
   Why do you think the artist gave it this title?

8.1 The right career?

Careers guidance questionnaire

1 Which of these areas can you see yourself working in?
Tick the boxes.

- ☐ business
- ☐ arts/entertainment
- ☐ education
- ☐ health and welfare
- ☐ media
- ☐ industry
- ☐ science/technology
- ☐ the environment
- ☐ politics/public life
- ☐ service industries

Other: ....

2 How true are these statements of you? Give yourself a mark out of five.

- ☐ I don't mind hard physical work.
- ☐ I enjoy working with my hands.
- ☐ I enjoy solving problems.
- ☐ I'm a good listener.
- ☐ I'm good with figures.
- ☐ I have a good artistic sense.
- ☐ I'm a good communicator.

3 Do you have any particular skills or leisure interests?

....
....
....
....
....

4 What are/were your favourite subjects at school?

....
....
....

5 What do you expect from a job? Give each of these a mark out of five.

- ☐ prospects for promotion
- ☐ the power to take your own decisions
- ☐ contact with other people
- ☐ a good salary
- ☐ the chance to travel
- ☐ long holidays
- ☐ being able to leave the job behind you when you go home

6 How true are these statements of you? Give each a mark out of 5.

- ☐ I get on with other people.
- ☐ I don't mind taking orders.
- ☐ I need to be my own boss.
- ☐ I go crazy if I do the same thing for too long.
- ☐ I can cope when things get tough.
- ☐ I like to look smart.
- ☐ I can keep smiling – however I'm feeling.
- ☐ I'm punctual.

DEATH BEGINS AT 40

Thanks to modern medicine, we live much longer than we used to. So no worries? Not quite. Once you're 40, the risk of serious illnesses like strokes, heart attacks and cancer begins to rise steeply. You'll probably survive – but will your income? You may have to stop working, or get a less strenuous job, or move home. So what will you do for money? It's a worrying thought.

Fortunately, here at the Insurance Union, we've thought of that. Our new Flexilife Policy is designed to protect you and your family while you recover from a serious illness. For a free brochure, phone us free on 000-0000-000 or send in the coupon below.

Insurance Union

We've got your interests at heart

E

STUDY or **Party?**

You can do both with *Energy Plus* caffeine tablets

Energy Plus WAKES YOU UP KEEPS YOU GOING

F

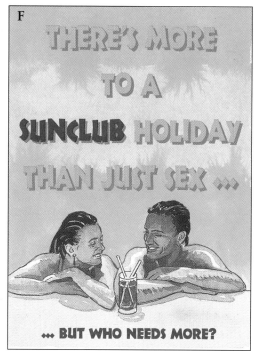

THERE'S MORE TO A SUNCLUB HOLIDAY THAN JUST SEX ...

... BUT WHO NEEDS MORE?

G

According to the BBC the world ends just after midnight

12.00 Weather
12.10 Close

MEGASAT TV

News, sport and movies. 24 hours a day, 7 days a week.

H

In just two weeks, YOU could be speaking fluent Italian.

Sounds incredible? But it's true, thanks to LinguComp's revolutionary LISTEN-AND-SAY method, which brings REAL ITALIAN into your home, your car or your workplace.

It's fun, it's easy, and it works!

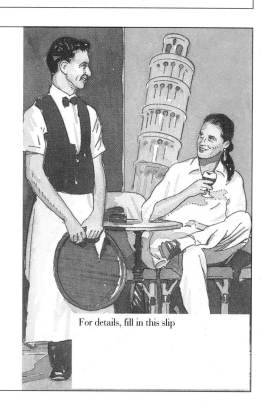

For details, fill in this slip

10.2 Science and the environment

For this study, conducted during 1993 and 1994, 25,000 adults in 20 countries were asked 12 true/false questions about science and the environment. The results, by country, are shown in the table.

The items that caused the most problems were:

– Item 8, about the greenhouse effect and the ozone layer (21% correct)
– Item 5, about man-made chemicals and cancer (36% correct)
– Item 3, about the scientific truth of astrology (44% correct).

ENVIRONMENTAL AND SCIENTIFIC KNOWLEDGE AROUND THE WORLD

A study conducted by the National Opinion Research Center at the University of Chicago

Rank	Country	Number correct
1	Canada	7.6
2	New Zealand	7.5
3	Great Britain	7.5
4	Norway	7.2
5	The Netherlands	6.8
6	Northern Ireland	6.7
7	USA	6.6
8	Germany (East)	6.6
9	Czech Republic	6.6
10	Germany (West)	6.4
11	Ireland	6.3
12	Japan	6.2
13	Italy	6.1
14	Israel	5.9
15	Hungary	5.8
16	The Philippines	5.6
17	Slovenia	5.5
18	Spain	5.3
19	Russia	4.8
20	Poland	4.3

14.1 Small but deadly *Aids*

What causes Aids?

Most scientists agree that Aids is caused by the HIV virus. The virus attacks the body's immune system, making the sufferer vulnerable to other diseases. It can be passed on by sexual contact, the use of shared needles for injecting drugs, and (now rarely) by blood transfusions using contaminated blood. It can also be passed on by pregnant women to their unborn children.

Symptoms

A person can be infected with HIV for many years with no symptoms at all, but in around 95% of cases Aids develops eventually. Since Aids sufferers have no defence against diseases in general, the symptoms can vary widely. They may include fever, weight-loss, infections of the mouth and, as the disease progresses, tuberculosis or leukaemia.

How widespread is it?

Aids is a relatively recent disease, but one which has spread rapidly around the world, particularly in Africa and in large cities in many countries. Estimates of the actual numbers involved vary widely.

Prevention

Avoid injecting drugs, particularly with a shared needle, and stick to one sexual partner. The use of condoms is known to reduce the risk of infection.

Cure

There is as yet no cure for Aids, which kills 99% of sufferers. Scientists have produced (and are producing) a number of drugs which slow down the progress of the disease, and there is a huge amount of research into finding out more about the disease. However, no effective vaccine has yet been developed.

HIV viruses emerging from a blood cell

11.3 Gadgets

make it (easier)
enable
prevent
stop
save
encourage
discourage

A

B

C

D

E

F

ただいま眠っております。
お手数ですが下記の駅で
起こしてください。

西荻窪   多謝

G

H

Inner peace

You're a calm, reflective and thoughtful person, and you're fascinated by hidden meanings and esoteric secrets. That's why you chose the Chinese character *tai*, which is painted on this egg. It symbolises deep inner peace.

What luck!

You have quite a superstitious nature, and you're secretly convinced that your fortune is in the hands of fate. So you naturally respond to the symbols of good fortune shown on this egg. You're optimistic and a positive thinker. Your motto is: if you believe everything will turn out well, then it will.

A quiet life

You're a naturally calm, placid person who longs for harmony and security and loves peace and quiet. You sometimes tend to be too easy-going and amenable, because you'd rather not face the fact that life isn't always quite as peaceful as you'd like it to be.

Lots of fun

You're a naturally cheerful, open and communicative person who likes to be sociable and to have a good time. You have a tendency to be a bit too talkative at times, but other people enjoy your company because you're such fun to be with!

Which way?

You tend to see life as a maze, full of problems and difficult decisions. You're a very sensitive person, sometimes a bit over-sensitive, with a desperate need for warmth and security. Other people sometimes find you difficult to be with, but they also find you fascinating.

What's new?

You're a naturally inquisitive person – you're interested in everything, especially what's going on on the other side of your garden fence! Although you've got an enquiring mind, you don't take things too seriously and you can also see the funny side of things and laugh at yourself. So although people find you a bit nosy, they enjoy your company.

Walking on air

Have you just fallen in love? Or have you just revived an old relationship? Certainly, if you chose this egg, you're feeling very light-hearted. Or maybe you just have a carefree, optimistic personality. Because you like yourself so much, other people find you attractive as well.

Burning with passion

You really throw yourself into life – sometimes a bit too aggressively. You're a natural fighter, dynamic, bold and passionate. You know exactly where you're going in life, and you'll do whatever's necessary to get there. Not surprisingly, you tend to make enemies, but people admire your courage and determination.

Yes, justice was done

I SEEM TO BE ONE of the few people that believe that Mr Newbery was wrong to shoot Mr Revill. As Mr Justice Rougier writes in a letter to today's *Times*, 'Those who believe that a home owner is entitled to shoot a burglar under any circumstances should ask themselves where this principle would end. Is a farmer entitled to shoot a boy stealing apples from his orchard? No? Then we have to strike a balance somewhere.'

Nobody doubts Mr Newbery's anger at the time, but he had planned the shooting, with the gun carefully placed behind a hole in the door. He fired at a range of five feet, which if not attempted murder was certainly extremely reckless.

Consider a similar incident, which took place last January in Houston, Texas. A householder, Jeffrey Agee, shot through the door at two men who were banging on it at four in the morning, killing one of them. In this case, the man was not a burglar but a Scotsman who had got lost and had wandered round the back of a house in search of help. The police did not press charges against Mr Agee. They took the view that his action was justified self-defence, as he could not have known that the men banging on his door were not burglars. As a Houston police spokesman said, 'You hear someone banging on your door like that, what are you going to do?'

The answer seems to be: shoot first and ask questions afterwards. Forget about gun control. An Englishman's allotment, like a Texan's veranda, is his castle. Strangers are guilty until proved innocent, and they had better prove it fast.

There is something seriously wrong about all this. Of course theft is a crime and housebreaking is a menace. But we make life less safe, not safer, by condoning private violence. As the American example shows us, letting people buy guns and use them as they like does not reduce violent crime, it increases it. There is no alternative to a proper police force actively patrolling the streets. There is no substitute for the rule of law. Vigilantes make easy media heroes. But in fact they are a menace to society.

1 What is the judge's point about stealing apples? Is it a fair comparison with what Mr Newbery did?

2 Why does the writer think Mr Newbery was wrong to do what he did?

3 Compare the incident in Texas with the one in England. In what ways
   – are they similar?   – are they different?

4 What is the writer's opinion of American gun laws?

14.1 Small but deadly *Malaria*

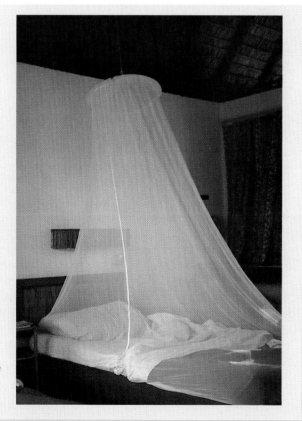

What causes malaria?
The disease is caused by the bite of the female anopheles mosquito, which passes the malarial parasite from one human to another.

Symptoms
The most obvious symptom is a high fever, but there can be other symptoms such as diarrhoea.

How widespread is it?
Malaria threatens over two billion people in 100 countries in the tropics. More than 100 million people catch the disease each year, and a million die from it, mainly children under five years old and pregnant women. In Africa, malaria kills around one child in 20.

Prevention
One way of preventing malaria is to eradicate the anopheles mosquito, but attempts to do this have not yet been successful. The other is to protect yourself by taking anti-malarial drugs wearing long-sleeved shirts and long trousers, using insect repellents and sleeping under mosquito nets. Unfortunately, in many places the malarial parasite has become resistant to anti-malarial drugs, and the problem is getting worse.

14.1 Small but deadly *Rabies*

What causes rabies?
Rabies is caused by a virus which affects the brain. It can affect all warm-blooded animals, and can be passed to humans through a bite by an infected animal.

Symptoms
At first, victims experience pain on swallowing; later, they become terrified of water, the very sight of which can cause paralysis. The patient eventually dies in a coma.

How widespread is it?
Most countries in the world have rabies, and in some countries it is a serious problem. In Thailand, 100,000 people a year need treatment after animal bites. One country with no rabies is Britain, which has strict controls on the entry of animals from other countries. There are fears that a rabid animal could enter Britain through the Channel Tunnel.

Prevention and cure
People (and their pets) can be vaccinated against rabies, and there have been attempts to vaccinate wild animals by putting out food containing the vaccine.

Once rabies has developed, there is no cure, but there is a treatment for people who have just been bitten. This is very unpleasant, and involves a course of 17 injections in the stomach wall.

14.1 Small but deadly *Cholera*

What causes cholera?
Cholera is caused by a bacterium, V. cholerae. A person can become infected by drinking water or eating food contaminated by the bacterium.

Symptoms
Diarrhoea and vomiting.

How widespread is it?
There are cholera outbreaks every year in different parts of the world. They are most common in places with unsafe water supplies and poor sanitation.

Prevention
Drink only water that has been boiled or treated with chlorine or iodine. Ice (and ice-cream) made with untreated water can also lead to infection. Only eat food that has been cooked and is still hot when served. Avoid raw seafood and other raw food except fruit and vegetables that you have peeled yourself.
Keep flies off your food – they may have been in contact with infected materials.

Cure
Cholera can be treated by antibiotics, but the real danger is death by dehydration, which can happen in a matter of only a few hours. The most important treatment is therefore rehydration – putting back the water that has been lost. Patients should drink a large amount of water mixed with oral rehydration salts (ORS). In more serious cases, where patients cannot hold down liquid, this can be given via a drip (see illustration). Rehydration treatment will save the lives of nearly all cholera patients.

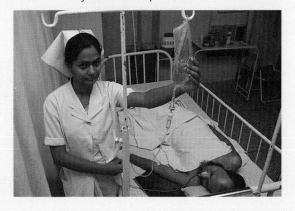

Macbeth – a synopsis

Act 1

RETURNING FROM BATTLE against the King of Norway, two Scottish generals Macbeth and Banquo meet three witches. They greet Macbeth as Thane of Glamis, Thane of Cawdor and King of Scotland. Macbeth is puzzled: he is Thane of Glamis, but the Thane of Cawdor is someone else, and Macbeth's cousin Duncan is King of Scotland.

Shortly afterwards, they find out that the Thane of Cawdor is dead. King Duncan makes Macbeth Thane of Cawdor in his place, and says he will soon be visiting Macbeth at his castle. So the witches were right about one thing. Were they right about the other too? Macbeth sends a message home to his wife, telling her what has happened.

When she gets the news, Lady Macbeth is determined that her husband will become King, and by the time Duncan arrives at the castle with his sons, she has persuaded Macbeth that they must murder him.

Act 2

That night, they drug the guards outside Duncan's bedroom, stab him to death while he is asleep, and smear his blood over the guards. Their hands are covered with blood, and Macbeth is horrified by what they have done. Lady Macbeth calms him down – 'A little water clears us of this deed,' she says – and gets him to bed.

Early next morning, Macduff, the Thane of Fife, arrives to collect Duncan. He finds the King dead, and Macbeth runs into the room and kills the guards. The King's sons, afraid that they will be killed too, run away. Everyone thinks that they arranged the murder of their father, and Macbeth is crowned King of Scotland.

Act 3

Macbeth is worried about Banquo. He is the only other person who knows about the witches – what if he is suspicious? He invites Banquo to a banquet, and has him murdered while he is out riding. At the banquet, Banquo's ghost appears. Only Macbeth can see it, and he is terrified. Lady Macbeth tells the guests her husband is ill, and they all go home.

Other people begin to get suspicious. Tormented by guilt and fear, Macbeth visits the witches. They tell him that 'no man born of woman shall harm Macbeth'.

Act 4

Macbeth becomes even more cruel and tyrannical. When he hears that Macduff has gone to England to visit Duncan's elder son Malcolm, he sends soldiers to Macduff's castle to kill all his family and servants. Macduff hears the terrible news, and is determined to take revenge on Macbeth. They raise an army and march to Scotland.

Act 5

[Act Five begins with the sleepwalking scene – see page 75]

As the enemy army approaches the castle, Macbeth prepares for battle. Lady Macbeth kills herself, but Macbeth, sure that he cannot be hurt, rides out to meet the enemy, and finds himself face to face with Macduff.

'Come and fight!' he says. 'No man born of woman can harm me.' But Macduff was not 'born' in the normal way – he was delivered by Caesarian section. The witches have tricked Macbeth. Macduff kills him, and Malcolm becomes King of Scotland.

Tapescripts

1·2 Past experiences

We were in the Arctic. I was with an Inuit guide, and we were a long way above the Arctic Circle. I was taking photographs of seals under water. And the weather had turned bad, so we had decided to spend the night on the ice. So there I was early in the morning, lying in the tent, just waking up, when I felt something moving against my feet. I looked to see what it was, and I could see the shape of a polar bear outside – it was playing with my feet through the wall of the tent. I kept as still as I could, and very quietly woke my Inuit guide and told him what was happening. He said, 'Don't worry. Just stick your head out of the tent and it'll go away.' So I said, 'Well, you stick *your* head out of the tent.' And he did – he stuck his head out of the tent, and sure enough the polar bear went away.

2·3 Learning a language

1 I work in American firm. It is transnationality company. We had, we have had office in Germany because we also a Germany firm. It is, it firm manufactured medical equipment. I work as advi– … scientist adviser for medicine and sale manager.

2 And they are so really nice family, they are taking well of me at least, and with … There's also other two people also with this family, they are students. And it's nice, it's nice for living, for managing your life here, so there is no difficulties at all. But especially because it's also the weather everywhere now it's winter time, and it's cold and windy. And, but it's good that it's, there is heat inside the classes, inside the public transportation, inside the home itself. So you feel warm, a little bit.

3 When is Saturday I go to, usually I go to cinema with my friend, my boyfriend, or I, or I go to the restaurant, usually. In the Sunday I don't make, or I make nothing of especial, I stay in my house with my parents, or I stay with my sister, or I study because I am a researcher and study is important for me. I read the article for my job, this, but I don't make a lot of things in the weekend.

4 My family. First my landlady, Fiona, and my landlord, Tony, and they have two children. The one is Carmen, she is five, yes, she is just five years old, and Chloe she just nine, nine month, yeah, old, and very lovely. And Tony is black man, so their skin's black, between black and white and very lovely, pretty, yeah. So I often play with them.

2·4 The truth about lying

1 Sometimes I lie to my husband, normally about the cost of things. This Christmas I bought my grandmother a silver photo frame to frame a picture of her great-grand-children. And the only one that I could find that I really liked happened to be a solid silver one, that was £65, and I told my husband it was silver-plated and it was £6.50. And he didn't notice of course, just looked at it quickly and then it was wrapped up and given to her, and she greatly appreciated it and thought it was wonderful. Of course nobody else knew that I'd spent that much money on it, but I felt that as it could be her last Christmas it was justified.

2 Quite recently I got married and my mother sent me an engraved plate with a little horse and carriage in the Victorian style and I personally hated this plate but I had to pretend that I was thrilled to bits with it, that it was one of the nicest things I could possibly receive, because I knew that my mother would be very hurt if I reacted in any other way.

3 I probably lie mainly to my parents, because they're very over-protective. I find myself lying about school and if I've done my homework. They always want me to be involved in extra activities, and so once I lied and told them I was in orchestra, and I carried this lie on for about six weeks or something. And eventually there was meant to be a concert, and they found out and, you know, it was just all hell broke loose basically, and I got in big trouble.

4 Quite recently somebody showed me a sample of curtain fabric that I thought was really awful, and I just didn't comment too much about it. I said I liked it, I said I thought it would go well in the room, which it would because I didn't like the room either.

5 I'm a teacher and in the course of my work pupils have to produce lots of coursework, and quite often it's necessary for me to lie to those pupils to encourage them to produce work of a better quality. For example, one of my pupils produced a small bike, push-along bike for his baby sister, quite recently. Now the quality of the bike wasn't very good but had I said to him 'That's rubbish' he would have been demoralised and given up. But by encouraging him to think that the work is excellent, he's gone on to produce excellent work.

6 When I was about seven, my sister would have been eleven and my brother was nine, and one Saturday afternoon we were going to be taken to the pictures. We had to have lunch first, and just before lunch I was very hungry, so I stole a banana. And I hid the skin behind a sewing machine in the dining room. My mother found it and asked us who had taken the banana. And I lied and I said it wasn't me. My sister looked terribly guilty for some reason, and my mother kept saying 'It was you, wasn't it? It was you.' And Pam looked more and more guilty, and eventually she got so upset that she couldn't go to the pictures, and I went off and I saw my Walt Disney film with my brother and I had my ice-cream and my popcorn and I have to say I didn't feel guilty at all.

A Double meanings

1 How did the farmer know his pony had a cold? (I don't know.) Because it was a little hoarse.

2 Why couldn't the tennis player light his cigarette? (I don't know.) Because he kept losing his matches.

3 Who won the race, the Malaysian or the Filipino? (Who?) Neither. It was a Thai.

4 Why can't leopards escape from the zoo? (I don't know.) Because they're always spotted.

5 What is the fastest thing in the universe? (I don't know.) Milk, because it's pasteurised before you even see it.

6 What's the difference between a cat and a comma? (I don't know) One's got claws at the end of its paws, and the other's a pause at the end of a clause.

A Intonation and meaning

Part 2

1. A It might be useful to meet and talk about it.
   B Mmm. How about 2 o'clock?
2. A ... and the pains started a few weeks ago?
   B Yes, that's right. About three weeks.
   A Three weeks. Mmm. Right, perhaps you could just lie down now, and I'll examine you ...
3. A I don't suppose you want to go out tonight?
   B Mmm. I'd love to.
4. A So I went to see John ...
   B Mmm.
   A And I told him what I'd decided ...
   B Mmm.
5. A Do you like Thai food?
   B Mmm. As long as it's not too spicy.
6. A Here's a present for you.
   B Mmm. Belgian chocolates!

3·3 Emphasising the point

1. Yeah, weekends are really important to me, because I'm with people all the week, and working very hard, and Sunday's really the only day that I have to myself, and so I really enjoy just getting up late and listening to the radio, wandering round the house. And the thing I really enjoy is reading the Sunday papers in bed. You can just sit there and read and you don't have to get up. Just drink coffee. It's wonderful.
2. I don't think I have any big problems with it and the tenses are no problem and I think I can manage very well but what I find really difficult is phrasal verbs, especially the ones with three words like 'put up with' or 'make up for' something. I think they're really difficult.
3. No it's great, all these fantastic tall skyscrapers, and so busy, people kind of everywhere and lots and lots going on. But the thing that really surprised me about New York was the way the shops stay open all night. You know, any time of the day or night you could go in and buy anything you wanted, four o'clock in the morning, made no difference
4. So I tried ringing the manager quite a few times and was blocked by his secretary each time, which was bad enough, but the thing that really annoyed me was that he never answered my letters, and I found that infuriating.

4·1 Dangerous pastimes

Part 1

A So, Alison, here we are at the airfield. You're about to go and do your first ever parachute jump. (Yes) How're you feeling?
B I'm excited, very very excited, and I'm prepared.
A Glad to hear that. Are you not just a little bit frightened?
B No, not frightened. I am a little nervous, because it's my first time, but I am looking forward to it.
A Good. Tell me, what, what made you decide to do it in the first place?
B Well, some friends of mine have been doing it for a while and they asked me if I'd like to join them and at first I said no but then I decided that, yes, I'm an adventurous type, and they sponsored me to do a jump for charity, so I said 'Fine, why not?' It's a good cause.
A Right. And you know what to do, do you? I mean, have you trained, have you practised?
B Oh yes, yes, yes. They make sure that you're well trained, they wouldn't let you up there if not, and we actually trained for a whole weekend.
A Right, whole weekend. What do you do? I mean, could you take us through it?
B Oh sure. Let's see, you jump, hopefully, and then the parachute's supposed to open, which it does after about four seconds, and if it doesn't you've got a reserve parachute, (Right) and then the second thing is that you have to land properly, so you just bend your knees, roll over when you land, you know.
A And you've learned all that by heart, have you?
B I sure hope so.
A Well don't worry, if you forget, I'll be there to catch you, all right? (Oh thank you) Good luck.
B OK, see you on the ground.

Part 2

A So congratulations. (Oh, thanks) How was it?
B Whew! Well, it was fantastic, really just fantastic.
A And what was it like? What did it feel like jumping out?
B Oh well at first I didn't want to jump out, but I was, I was kind of forced to, which I'm glad, because it was just unlike anything I've ever done before. (I'm sure) You kind of, I don't know, there's this rushing sensation, and then that parachute opens, and then you feel in control because you just slow right down, and that's when,

that's when
wasn't at fir
superb.
A Great. And i
there were n
parachute?
B No, thank goo
Oh – the landi   ...t so
great. I landed ... but I forgot to get
up, which they did warn us about,
and I was dragged across the ground
a little bit, but – no problem.
A The million dollar question. Do you think you'll go again?
B Yes, yes, yes, definitely. (Good) Yes.

4·4 Problems, problems ...

Problem 1: In the post
Clue 1: Well you can't actually make the sword shorter, so you have to make it *seem* shorter.
Clue 2: Supposing she used a box that wasn't too long, but was a bit wider.
Answer: OK, what she did was she got a box 95 centimetres long, but one that was also fairly wide. And then she didn't put the sword in straight, she put it in diagonally.

Problem 2: Two boyfriends
OK, well this is all to do with the times of the trains, and the point is that the train in Bill's direction always comes one minute later than the one in Mario's direction, right? So if you imagine that Mario's train comes at 9 minutes past the hour, and Bill's train comes at 10 past – obviously she's only ever going to see Bill if she happens to get to the station in that one minute between 9 and 10 past.

Problem 3: An explosive mixture
The main problem is with boxes D and E, because they each touch six other boxes. So you start with them, and you put bottles 1 and 8 in D and E. Then you put bottles 7 and 2 in C and F. And once you've done that, the rest of it's easy.

Problem 4: Sweet revenge
Well in fact you only have to move one jar. All you have to do is pick up the second jar, tip all the sweets into the fifth jar, and then put it back again.

Problem 5: One man and his dog
Well after the farmer lets the dog off the lead he walks another 20 km. And since the dog's running three times as fast as the farmer, obviously he'll go three times the distance in the same time. So the answer's 60 km.

Problem 6: On balance
Well in fact he only needs to make two weighings. What he does is, he divides the boxes into three groups, with three boxes in each group, right? Then he

the groups together. If ...'s heavier, that's where the ... are. If they weigh the same, ... the diamonds must be in the group ... hasn't weighed yet. OK – now he knows which group the diamonds are in. So all he has to do is take that group and do the same thing again. He takes two of the boxes and weighs them. And that tells him which box the diamonds are in.

Problem 7: Whodunnit?
A and B contradict each other, so one of them must be lying and one must be telling the truth. Now we know there are two liars, so C must be lying as well. So when C says 'I'm innocent' we know he must be lying – so the answer's C.

Problem 8: Wrong labels
Now you have to concentrate a bit on this one – the point is that *all* the labels on the sacks are wrong. So what he should do is take a potato out of the sack marked 'mixed'. OK, let's say it's a white potato. Then that must be the sack with the white potatoes. So what's in the sack marked 'red'? It can't be red (because we know the label's wrong), and it can't be white – so it must be mixed. So that just leaves the sack marked 'white' – and obviously that must contain the red potatoes.

B Conversational remarks

Part 1
1 There, there.
2 See you.
3 Now then.
4 Do you see?
5 Cheers!
6 Come off it.

Part 2
1 A They took my money, my credit cards, my passport, everything.
  B Oh dear. What are you going to do now?
2 They can't just come to me and tell me I can't work for them any more. I mean, it's just not on.
3 A Get on with it. We haven't got all day.
  B OK. I've just got to finish this – I'll be ready in a minute.
4 A But she's got a university degree.
  B So what? You've had more experience – that's what counts.
5 A I'm not really sure if I can come out this evening. I've got so much to do.
  B Well, it's up to you. But let me know what you decide, OK?
6 A What's up? You look up awful.
  B Oh, I've just got a bit of a headache, that's all.

7 A What was his phone number?
  B No idea. Look it up in the book.
8 A Whoops, sorry.
  B Watch where you're going.
  A Sorry. Are you OK?
9 A Phew! That was close.
  B Yeah – maniac.

5·2 Difficult situations

1 I was returning from America, flying into Heathrow Airport, and I was bringing back a diet powder for a friend, and it looked suspiciously like a drug powder. And I was pulled aside by the people at customs, and they found this, and I must confess it did look very suspicious because I had it taped up and it looked very much like drugs. And they took it aside to be tested in a side room and they strip-searched me and went through every item of clothing I had. And they kept accusing me of bringing in what was I mean almost about five pounds of cocaine. Ultimately, they did do a quick test on it and they found that it was just fructose powder, and they released me with a stern warning.

2 I was driving home from work one afternoon down a one-way street to my home, and parked in front of me was a removal van, and it had the back doors of the removal van open so that they could take the furniture and stuff out. And I drove up and tooted my horn, expecting somebody to close one of the doors so that I could drive past. And as I tooted my horn, this huge bloke emerged from behind the door with a crowbar in his hand, and threatened to smash my windscreen unless I backed off. Well, I was in a one-way street, but he was sufficiently threatening for me to actually put the car into reverse and go the wrong way up the one-way street and find another way home.

3 When I was about ten years old I had an argument with a girl in my class. And about a week later the headmistress called me into her office for something, I didn't know what it was. So I went in there, and she told me that I was going to be put in detention for scratching my name in the table. I didn't know anything about this, so I asked her to show me. She took me into the classroom, and sure enough my name was scratched into the table. There was nothing I could do about it. Anyway, the actual girl that I had the argument with finally admitted to me that she'd scratched my name in the table. But there was no way that I

could prove it to the headmistress, so I just had to pay the penalty.

6·2 What needs doing?

1 OK, well I'll have to go and take a look outside because I think there's probably a tile missing from the roof, in which case that will have to be replaced, and it will mean repainting inside on the ceiling.
2 Right, we'll just have to see how big the hole is. We'll be able to repair it if it's not too bad; otherwise we might have to replace the whole inner tube.
3 Right, you'll have to put a new pane of glass in, and part of the frame might have to be replaced as well. All that paint will need scraping off, and then you'll have to repaint it.
4 Right, I'll see if I can get the stain out. It might have to go to the dry cleaner's. I can sew the tear up, that's no problem, and I can sew the button back on, that's easy enough as well.
5 Well, you could try sticking the handle back on again with superglue. But then I wouldn't carry anything too heavy in it or it might come off again.

6·4 They did it themselves

A So Philippe, you're about to open a new restaurant called the Tarte Flambée. Where did you get the idea from?
B The idea comes from Alsace. It's a thin dough of bread which is used to be cooked about 200 years ago by the peasants and they used to roll the bread very thin and put ingredients they had at hand, which was bacon, fromage frais, and they used to put it into the oven and cook it very fast to show them if the oven was hot enough to cook the bread.
A So it was a kind of very old-fashioned fast food, in fact.
B Yes, it was the ancestor of the pizza, really, because originally the pizza was made with bread dough, a peasant dish, which is cheap ingredients, fast to cook, not expensive to eat. And also primarily communal eating, fun, you know, eating as a group of people.
A So your idea is to introduce this as a new kind of restaurant in England, yeah?
B Well, we thought there was a market for sort of good fast food, that it would be a good idea to introduce a simple food, it's not as filling as a pizza is, it's as tasty, moister, and it's cheaper. So as long as we can keep this equation right, then we should

be able to make a success.

A So are you planning to have take-away as well as people eating at the restaurant?

B Yes, eventually we are planning to also put them into little boxes and people can come and have some take-away as well. But primarily we want to make a restaurant which is very characteristic of a cheap bistro-style in France, you know, where you eat around the table, you have the food in the middle, you are cutting it and you have a bit of music around and it's fun and relaxed and not at all like a formal gastronomic restaurant where you have waiters looking at you, you know, in a formal way and filling up your glass of wine every five minutes, you know. This one is much more of a bistro, peasant, I would say, type of eating.

A I mean in England now we've got, if you go to any high street we have pizza parlours and burger places and fried chicken places and baked potatoes. What makes you think that tarte flambée will be as successful as pizza?

B Well the ingredients are fresh and it tastes great I think. And also, primarily you eat it in a group. So you have it in the middle of the table like I was saying, and it's a social occasion, much more than having your own little baked potato or your own little pizza in front of you. This goes in the middle of the table, you cut it in four or six and you're all eating it and when you've finished you have another one. And you don't have to decide, you know, before your meal starts, you don't have to decide how much you want, you can decide that at the time you're eating it, so if you eat one and you feel full, you stop, if you want another one you ask for another one, you know, and it takes two and a half minutes to cook.

A So, when do you open?

B Well we're opening on Friday night, so that's going to be our first night, everybody's very excited about it, so all the staff is eager to start now, and we hope for the best.

A Well, I'll be there. Thank you very much. Good luck.

B Thank you.

C British and US English

Part 1

There's a story of a young Englishman who was staying with a couple in New York. It was his first time in the United States, and on the first night, they had dinner and they were looking forward to going out to see a play on Broadway. After dinner the wife got up and said 'Well, I think I'll just wash up'. Well the Englishman immediately sprang to his feet and said 'Oh let me help'. Well, of course everyone just burst out laughing.

Part 3

Grammar is another area where things can be a little different between American English and British English. One of those areas is with the use of prepositions. For example, we would say *on the weekend* whereas in Britain it's *at the weekend*.

With days of the week we often leave the preposition out altogether. So an American will say *See you Tuesday* rather than the British *See you on Tuesday*.

And then there are some verbs where British people use a preposition but Americans don't. So in Britain people *protest against high taxes*, whereas in America, you simply *protest high taxes*. Likewise, in America you *write someone* and in Britain you *write to someone*.

Another thing I've noticed is that in Britain people say *I like swimming* or *I love watching TV*. Americans prefer to use the infinitive: *I like to swim, I love to watch TV*.

And there's a tense difference too with verbs. Where in Britain people say, for example, *I've already seen him* or *He hasn't come yet*, Americans will often use the Past tense instead: *I already saw him, He didn't come yet*.

And also, in America the past participle of *get* can be *gotten* rather than *got* – so an American will say *I've gotten the tickets* rather than *I've got the tickets*. Those are some of the main differences.

7·3 How do you picture it?

Interpretation 1

There is a girl in the middle sitting at a table. Her face looks open and without any particular expression. She seems to be looking in front of her as if she was waiting for something to happen. Behind her there is a young man. He looks like Andy Warhol. He's also looking in the same direction as the girl as if they were posing for a photograph, saying 'We belong together. We come from the same world.' Behind them there seems to be a screen. There is a third face coming through the screen, with the face of a man who's probably coming from the Third World. He looks hungry and he's looking hungrily at this bowl of soup in front of the girl. Well, I'm not sure what this picture is about. One thing might be a criticism of society, that some people in the Western world have too much of consumer goods and that there are people in the world who are still very hungry.

Interpretation 2

Well, in the centre of this picture there is a young woman, who also I think looks a little bit like a schoolgirl. And the table she's sitting at looks a bit like a school desk. And she seems to be sitting there waiting to be told what to do, or listening to the two people who are behind her. And these two people behind her seem to represent different sides of herself. And on one side there is a man who looks like Andy Warhol, and he looks very sophisticated, very beautiful. And this is the side that she wants to copy, I think. She's got the same hair as he has, they're wearing the same glasses, they're looking in the same direction. And behind her on the other side there is another figure, an older woman, who appears to be pushing her way into the picture from behind. And I think this woman represents another side of herself, a much darker side, she is much more primitive, she's older. And she is not as beautiful as Andy Warhol, of course, but she is much more alive, and she's also much bigger and more powerful in the picture. And perhaps this is the hidden side of herself, which is trying to force its way into her consciousness, and which perhaps she doesn't want to recognise.

8·2 Success story

It's an incredible success story. It was this man Chris Anderson, he was working for a company who produced a home computer magazine. Well, he had a row with his boss and he was sacked, so he decided to launch his own computer magazine. So what he did was, he got together with his wife and a couple of friends, and started a company called *Future Publishing*. Well, they set up an office in his bedroom at home, and they took out a bank loan of about £15,000 and launched their own computer magazine called *Amstrad Action*. Well, the first issue they did, they didn't even sell enough copies to break even, but they kept going and the next issue made a profit and they managed to pay off the original bank loan after just three months. And then after that they just expanded and expanded, they took on more staff and they launched other computer titles, like *PC Plus* for example. They kept adding other magazine titles, on all other sorts of topics like needlework and mountain biking and all kinds of things. Apparently, their turnover now has risen by about 90 per cent a year ever since, and now they've got more than 30 different magazine titles. Eventually Chris Anderson decided to sell the company, and he got something incredible like £50 million for it. He went off to the States and now doing it all over again.

8.4 Dirty money

Part 1

A In the past week, a number of small businesses in Britain have received a fax which promises to make them rich. The fax apparently comes from a top employee in a foreign oil company, who wants to transfer funds out of his country into a British bank account. Alex Clarke, who runs a small software company in London, is one of those who received the fax.

B Well, they claimed that they had 32 million American dollars which they wanted to transfer into my company bank account. According to them all they, I all had to do, rather, was to send them details of the bank account, obviously, and some headed notepaper, headed company notepaper, and that was it basically, the money would be transferred. In return for that we would receive 30 per cent of that money, which comes to a total of very nearly $10 million.

A It sounds like an offer you can't refuse. So was Mr Clarke tempted to do as he was asked?

B I was certainly very much tempted, I mean it's a great deal of money, as you can see, but one of the rules of business is you don't get something for nothing and this really did seem to be too good to be true. And I was a little bit suspicious about a couple of things. Firstly, they did openly and freely admit in the fax that the money was stolen, and secondly, for some reason which they didn't specify, they said they wanted the whole thing kept totally secret.

A So Mr Clarke gave up the chance of a lifetime, and instead sent a copy of the fax to the police. Now I have Inspector John Markham ...

Part 2

A ... to the police. Now I have Inspector John Markham of the Metropolitan Police with me in the studio. Inspector Markham, good morning.

C Morning, Sue.

A So did Mr Clarke do the right thing, or did he miss out on a fortune?

C No no, he definitely did the right thing. This is actually a fraud, and happens quite a lot. If Mr Clarke had gone ahead, he certainly wouldn't

have gained any money, and he would probably have lost a lot.

A So how does the fraud work?

C Well, once they receive your company bank details and your headed notepaper, they can use these to transfer money out of your bank account. Now I'm not going to say how that's done, for obvious reasons. Very likely Mr Clarke would have gone to his bank account one day in a week or two's time and he'd have found it empty.

A Right, so he did do the right thing, then. (Yeah, certainly) But you say this kind of fraud is common. How common?

C Well, there are several cases a year. There was a similar case a few months ago, supposedly from the same oil company, but this time only offering $1.5 million. And before they were caught, these fraudsters had collected around £700,000.

A So is it only small businesses that get approached in this way?

C It is mostly, yes, yes, but it's also happened with charities. What happens is a charity receives a fax saying that somebody's died and has left them a large amount of money. Then later on the charity is asked for £5,000 to pay the death duties and that's the last you hear of them.

A Inspector Markham, thank you very much. (You're welcome) So if you run a small business – or a charity – and you receive a suspicious-looking fax which seems too good to be true, our advice is, sadly, to throw it in the bin or, better still, pass it on to the police.

9·3 Playing it safe

A They say that New York is pretty dangerous now, but are you actually likely to get mugged?

B Oh, you've seen too many movies. No, no. People exaggerate. As long as you're reasonably careful like in any major city of the world, you'll be OK. Of course, it depends upon what part of the city you're walking in.

A Right, that's interesting. Are there certain parts that are more dangerous than others?

B Oh yeah. I wouldn't go walking around in Harlem at the night time, especially if you're white. A stroll through Central Park after dark is not a good idea. Certainly you'll get mugged in there. But in Manhattan, which is really where most tourists go, stick to the main streets and you'll be fine. For instance, 42nd Street is fine. People think if they go to 41st Street or 43rd, because

they're side streets, it'll be safer, but actually there are no police there. So, stick to the main ones, 57th, 34th, 42nd, 14th and so forth.

A Right. So, be confident, be strong, is that the sort of thing?

B Abso–... Look like you belong there. Yeah. You know, tourists, they'll scream 'tourist' by the way they dress, they carry a map, they look at the tops of buildings, they stand on street corners obviously lost, they flash money about, they have too much jewellery. Don't do that. Look like a New Yorker. Walk like a New Yorker. Talk like a New Yorker if you can.

A Difficult. But we'll try. Thank you.

10·2 Science and the environment

This first one is false. We certainly produce some radioactivity, but there's also plenty of natural radiation around – this comes from cosmic rays hitting the Earth, and also from ancient rocks such as granite.

Number two is true. If you've got a cold (which is caused by a virus), it's absolutely no use taking antibiotics.

Three is false. A lot of people believe in astrology, of course – but there's no scientific explanation for how the position of stars or planets at the time of your birth could possibly affect your character. So astrology has no scientific basis.

Four: also true. This hasn't been proved conclusively, but all the evidence we have – fossil remains, and so on – points to evolution rather than any other explanation.

Five is false. Everything on the planet is chemical. Most man-made chemicals are neither more nor less harmful than natural ones.

Number six: false. We all come into contact with radioactivity, but we don't all die from it. On the other hand, radioactivity can certainly be dangerous, and no one really knows what a safe dose is.

Seven: that's true. In fact, some radioactive waste will remain dangerous for hundreds of thousands of years.

Eight: false. The greenhouse effect is caused by greenhouse gases like carbon dioxide, which prevent heat from escaping. The hole in the ozone layer is something completely different – it's the reason you should be careful when you're out in the sun.

Nine is true. Burning them produces carbon dioxide, which is the main greenhouse gas. Coal is the worst, by the way, then oil, and gas is the least harmful.

Number ten: false. Some pesticides are really dangerous, and many of those are now banned. There are some that may cause cancer if they're not used correctly – but certainly not all of them. Eleven true: We're destroying thousands of species a year. Some people believe that we're causing more extinctions than the ones that happened millions of years ago.

And twelve: false. They are one of the major causes of acid rain, and a major source of greenhouse gases – so they certainly do cause air pollution.

10·4 Science fiction

Part 1

The children were always good during the month of August, especially when it began to get near the twenty-third. It was on this day that the great silver spaceship carrying Professor Hugo's Interplanetary Zoo settled down for its annual six-hour visit to the Chicago area.

Before daybreak the crowds would form, long lines of children and adults both, each one clutching his or her dollar, and waiting with wonderment to see what race of strange creatures the Professor had brought this year.

In the past they had sometimes been treated to three-legged creatures from Venus, or tall, thin men from Mars, or even snakelike horrors from somewhere more distant. This year, as the great round ship settled slowly to earth in the huge tri-city parking area just outside of Chicago, they watched with awe as the sides slowly slid up to reveal the familiar barred cages. In them were some wild breed of nightmare – small, horselike animals that moved with quick, jerking motions and constantly chattered in a high-pitched tongue. The citizens of Earth clustered around as Professor Hugo's crew quickly collected the waiting dollars, and soon the good Professor himself made an appearance, wearing his many-coloured rainbow cape and top hat. 'Peoples of Earth,' he called into his microphone.

The crowd's noise died down and he continued. 'Peoples of Earth, this year you see a real treat for your single dollar – the little-known horse-spider people of Kaan – brought to you across a million miles of space at great expense. Gather around, see them, study them, listen to them, tell your friends about them. But hurry! My ship can remain here only six hours!'

And the crowds slowly filed by, at once horrified and fascinated by these strange creatures that looked like horses but ran up the walls of their cages like spiders. 'This is certainly worth a dollar,' one man remarked, hurrying away. 'I'm going home to get the wife.'

All day long it went like that, until ten thousand people had filed by the barred cages set into the side of the spaceship. Then, as the six-hour limit ran out, Professor Hugo once more took microphone in hand. 'We must go now, but we will return next year on this date. And if you enjoyed our zoo this year, phone your friends in other cities about it. We will land in New York tomorrow, and next week on to London, Paris, Rome, Hong Kong and Tokyo. Then on to other worlds!'

He waved farewell to them, and as the ship rose from the ground the Earth peoples agreed that this had been the very best Zoo yet …

Part 2

Some two months and three planets later, the silver ship settled at last onto the familiar jagged rocks of Kaan, and the queer horse-spider creatures filed quickly out of their cages. Professor Hugo was there to say a few parting words, and then they scurried away in a hundred different directions, seeking their homes among the rocks.

In one, the she-creature was happy to see the return of her mate and offspring. She babbled a greeting in their strange tongue and hurried to embrace them. 'It was a long time you were gone. Was it good?'

And the he-creature nodded. 'The little one enjoyed it especially. We visited eight worlds and saw many things.'

The little one ran up the wall of the cave. 'On the place called Earth it was the best. The creatures there wear garments over their skins, and they walk on two legs.'

'But isn't it dangerous?' asked the she-creature.

'No,' her mate answered. 'There are bars to protect us from them. We remain right in the ship. Next time you must come with us. It's well worth the nineteen commocs it costs.'

And the little one nodded. 'It was the very best Zoo ever …'

D Conversational fillers

Part 1

1 Well, I do like it, I mean really I know I shouldn't, but um, you know how it is, if you have one and you want another it's um, it's a bit difficult to stop, really.

2 I think it's a really um disgusting habit, really, and you know, you know if you're um in a restaurant or something and people start smoking, I think it's disgusting, basically, I think it's really awful.

3 Yeah, well I've been smoking now for, ooh I don't know, about 30 years or so I suppose, and I'm kind of smoking one year and kind of giving up the next, and um actually it's been going on like that for ages and um you know when I, when I give up I just put on all this weight. So I kind of give up, and then I get very depressed because I'm overweight, so I kind of um, so I take it up again.

Part 2

A Well, um, let me see, I think it was quite a small room, and um it had yellow wallpaper, I think, as far as I remember, and um yeah with pictures of penguins I think, or something like that.

B Well, you see, the fact is that I've been very very busy recently, and well, to be honest I haven't had time to look at it. And that's how it is really, it just can't be helped.

C Well, I was just thinking um, one possible idea might be um to um organise a sort of fancy dress party, or something like that. I mean, it's just an idea. What do you think?

D Well the fact is, I mean let's face it, the government isn't actually doing anything to improve the health service. In fact, if you ask me all they're really interested in doing is saving money. Well, that's how I see it, anyway.

11·1 For better, for worse

1 I think it's more difficult for young people these days. I think that people have to grow up so quickly, it's almost like, you know, your childhood is over and done with before you know it. And schools, you know, they cut back so much on education resources that schools are no longer really a fun place to be. So I find that a bit grim really, I don't see a lot of joy and happiness for young people and teenagers.

2 Well I think the streets actually are worse. Any kind of major city that you walk down, the place is completely filthy and there's a lot of homeless people around now and it's actually quite frightening and quite threatening. People are begging all the time. And it's just a nightmare going anywhere these days.

3 One area that I think has improved greatly is the variety of fruit and vegetables available in your local supermarket. You can now get about ten different sorts of lettuce and the varieties of tropical fruit that you can now buy are wonderful.

4 I think one of the ways things have changed for the worse, and I don't

know if this is just me and I'm getting older, but I do think there seems to be a greater sense of lawlessness and a lack of responsibility, especially among some young people, and you see kids doing things that you would never imagine seeing 20 years ago, smashing up trains and things in front of the other passengers, things like that. So I think that's a step backwards.

5 The great thing about the nineties for me really is package holidays, because they're so cheap, and you can fly anywhere around the world. Now when I was a kid, well I had one holiday abroad I think, and that wasn't because we were a particularly deprived family, but everything was just much more expensive then, and you didn't get the flights that you have now. Now you can nip down to your travel agent and book a flight for tomorrow and you're half way across the world.

6 One of the good things, though, I think about today is that there's a lot more choice around in terms of work and career, especially for women, I think there are more equal opportunities, there are women going into professions that, you know, 20, 30 years ago would be considered solely a male profession. So I think that that's a very encouraging thing about today's society.

7 Well, in my mind the way things have moved forwards best really in the last few decades is that in terms of foreigners in this country, people are far more accepting of them. Particularly when it comes to children, you know, in schools people are taught to respect other people's cultures, languages, religions.

8 The particular thing that I think has got much worse is overpowering perfumes. You can't walk into a restaurant or a pub or a café without getting attacked by four or five different sorts of stinks, really, and men I'm afraid have also sort of jumped on the bandwagon and this is a trend that I think should definitely be discouraged.

12·2 Relationships

1 I think total honesty with each other, communication – if you can talk about anything and discuss things and you're totally honest about what you want and what you feel, you can't go wrong.

2 I think mutual interests are very important in a relationship. If a couple comes together with mutual interests in something like the theatre and sports and they enjoy the same type of people, then it's a wonderful ground for this couple to make new friends, to laugh together, and through this kind of communication I think a relationship really grows and flowers.

3 One of the important things in a relationship for me is a beautiful partner, because I like to feel proud when I go out, it's nice to have somebody good on your arm, and it rubs off on me. People think 'There's a beautiful couple.'

4 I think a relationship should be about a partnership between close friends and that you should be allowed to lead your own lives within the partnership and have your own friends and your own interests.

5 Well, what I first look for is probably good looks, because at my age it's not going to be such a serious relationship, and so you just like to be with someone who looks good.

6 I think it's very important to be able to admit that you've made a mistake once in a while, and it's also very important I think generally not to take yourself too seriously in relation to the other person.

7 For me the most important thing in a relationship is love. And this means taking the other person as he is and also leaving him the space he wants.

12·4 Skin deep

A You run a tattoo studio in quite a small town. Do you get a lot of business?

B Yes, we do. My clientele basically can come from anywhere from sort of local people up to I get people coming over from Europe, I get visitors from Holland, from all over the place, we do. Yes.

A And what kind of people come for tattoos, I mean, are things changing?

B You could say that. It could be anyone from society, basically; over the last ten years it's become a lot more popular and a lot more acceptable.

A Do you get women, a lot of women coming in?

B I would say probably 50 per cent of the clientele that comes through the studio is female.

A What kind of tattoos do people usually ask for?

B Well, nowadays it can be anything, but the traditional tattoos, the hearts, flowers, roses and daggers, that sort of thing is still quite popular, but we do a lot more of art stuff as well, portrait work and reproduction work.

A Has anybody ever asked you for anything really unusual?

B I think basically if you can think of it we've probably tattooed it at some stage.

A You're talking about parts of the body now, are you?

B Yes and also what can be tattooed on someone. Basically if something can be drawn it can be tattooed, and it really is as simple as that.

A So once you have a tattoo, is that it, you've got your tatoo, or do people come back for more?

B I tend to find that if someone comes in and they have a tattoo done, it can be the first of many. There's a couple of people that that I know, that live in the local area, that have actually become friends, we've got to know each other over the years. I've got a chap who comes in from Devizes and he started off just with a couple of tattoos but now he's wearing a tattoo that is nearly 80 per cent of his body is covered and it's turned into a three-dimensional picture of a castle basically, so as you walk around his body you're looking through the different windows at the scenes that are actually taking place inside. And that, we've been tattooing Winnie for the last five years on a fortnightly basis.

A I see you've got a notice outside warning people that tattoos are permanent and telling them to think about it first. Do you find that's necessary?

B I think so, yes, 'cause someone can come into the studio and there can be a case of 'Oh I like that design, I want that now', spur of the moment, but people do have to realise that it is something that is there for life. Basically the only thing it can be swapped for is a scar. What I tend to do, if I'm not happy that the client is not going to be happy with the tattoo I will not tattoo them, it's as simple as that.

A So you have refused to tattoo people (Yes) who want tattoos?

B Yeah, especially with certain placements, especially with tattoos that are going to be placed on the face or the hands, we just will not do it.

A Now I see a lot more people with tattoos these days than I used to. It's clearly becoming more popular. Do you see a time when tattooing will be a normal thing to do, when you can walk in your local department store, maybe, and there's a tattoo studio in there?

B I don't think so, no. Tattooing has always had a taboo that's sort of gone with it. I think that the idea of walking into somewhere like Debenhams and just getting tattooed I don't think'll happen, somehow.

A So you don't see someone like Princess Diana going out with a tattoo on her arm?

B Well, I mean to be perfectly honest, I mean the Royal Family back in the early 19th century were heavily tattooed themselves. Yes.

E Regional accents

1 I had a very very happy childhood. I was brought up on the coast, in this lovely little seaside town, and you know so there was always plenty to do there, like you know on the weekends or after school. You could go down the beach, and play on the rocks. A really, really lovely place to live, I think.

2 Well, the thing I always remember about the weekend, right, is that my old man had a bit of work on the side, I mean he had the job during the week, you know, but he needed to do something else at the weekend to make ends meet. So he used to a little bit of catering, he used to do, like, weddings and parties, things like that, you know.

3 I grew up on a farm, and one thing about that is you tend not to have many playmates, and so therefore I was sort of limited in that I could only really play with my brother, my sister was too small at the time. And it's a kind of wonderful world for children to grow up when you grow up in the countryside, and all your games are all based out in the fields or down the woods, and you just invent all the time, because obviously I think that you've got these wonderful places to explore, so I mean our woods became the jungle and wonderful rich forests.

4 I always hated my cousin Linda. She was a year younger than me, but she always got me in trouble. And I remember one day we were visiting grandma, and Linda said to me, 'Let's go see Auntie Sal because she's got candy.' And so off we went, and our parents hadn't realised we'd gone missing. And they sent the neighbours out searching for us and all my relatives. And one of our uncles, Uncle George, finally found us, and put us in his car to take us back, and when we got home, I was punished, my mother spanked me.

5 We used to really like going down to the harbour because there was so much going on down there. There was a little bay, and a boat used to be down there. It was tied up, I don't know who owned it, but we used to sort of borrow it, it wasn't stealing, we just borrowed it, you know. And we'd all pile into it, there'd be two or three girls, a couple of dogs, we used to have an oar to row – one oar to row with, and that was it, we used to go heading out on the harbour. And it was pretty deep, it was pretty dangerous, but you know we used to love it, it was great fun.

6 Well, I was at boarding school when I was a child, all girls. And my best friend was Sarah, Sarah Woolley. And I was thrilled to bits when she invited me for half term to stay with her family. And she lived near the coast, and from her bedroom you could see the sea. And I thought that was just wonderful.

7 I've got two brothers, and they're twins. I remember as children we were always fighting, especially my two brothers over something or nothing. But the three of us, we used to be in a gang. But there was another gang as well, and with these two gangs we used to have rival fights and throwing stones at each other. It was a really roughish neighbourhood, you could say, and you really had to be tough and ready to go.

13·3 Speaking your mind

1 A Oh, by the way, they're not coming after all.
  B What? You could have told me earlier. I've just spent the last three hours getting the place sorted out.

2 Don't you ever run out into the road like that again. You could have been knocked over.

3 A Well, that was awful. What a waste of time. Why did we bother?
  B I don't know. Couldn't believe it. Frozen pizza. I mean, we might just as well have stayed at home and had a take-away.

4 A Everything ready?
  B Yes, no thanks to you.
  A Why, what do you mean?
  B Well, you might have offered to lend a hand, instead of just sitting there reading the paper.

5 *Newsreader:* … in the semi-final of the World Cup, New Zealand defeated England by 45 points to 25.
  Viewer: Oh, I might have known. As soon as we come up against a really good side, we lose.

6 Look, I know they were pretty boring, I know they were going on and on, but you needn't have been quite so rude. I mean, what was I to say? I was so embarrassed.

7 For me? Oh, you needn't have bothered. But they're lovely. Thank you so much.

14·2 Medical treatment

1 Will you roll up your sleeve, please. Here you go. Be very quick. There we are. All finished.

2 Right, I'm just going to put this over here. There we are. OK, I'm just going out of the room for a minute. Um, all you've got to do is keep absolutely still. OK?

3 A Mm-hmm. Mm. Oh. Yep. Here's one. One small cavity. Listen, I can fill it right away if you like. You probably want an injection.
  B Oh, no, I don't, thank you. I don't like them.

4 Oh that's a bad cut isn't it. We'll have to do something about that. Right, sit still, I'll just put some cream on it first, it doesn't sting (Ooh) – it's all right. There we are. Now just put this on. There we are. Sit still. There we are.

5 OK, I'm going to make an incision above the left ventricle. Scalpel, please, nurse. Thank you. OK.

6 I'll give you two lots to keep you going. There we are. That's two tablets three times a day, OK? And if that doesn't do the trick, come back next week.

7 OK, open your mouth. Good. Now close your mouth. Keep it under your tongue – Oop, don't bite it. That OK? (Mmm) Good.

14·3 Alternative medicine

Well the first teaching job I had I was teaching at a secondary school in West Africa. And this school was way out in the bush, a long long way from the nearest town. And it was a fairly kind of dusty area, the school, and very few of the boys had shoes and most used to walk around with bare feet. And there were scorpions in the area, and almost every day one or other of the students would get a scorpion sting. Now these scorpions weren't fatal but the bite was, the sting was very very painful and if it wasn't treated it would keep you in bed for a week, you wouldn't be able to walk for a week. And the usual thing to do was to go down to the hospital, which was one of the few parts of the town that had electricity, and the hospital would give you an injection and that would help the pain, and after say two or three days you'd be able to get up and walk around again and resume lessons. But many of the students at the school preferred to go to a traditional doctor, and now and again I would be asked to take a student with a scorpion sting down to this doctor on my motorbike. And the treatment that the traditional doctor would give the patient was extraordinary, it was completely different from anything else that I've ever seen. The first thing he used to do was to mix up a very kind of muddy looking liquid which the student would drink. And then there'd be some kind of chanting from the traditional doctor, and he would start with his fingers on the affected foot and would chant all the time and move his fingers gradually up the student's leg, up his body, and then along his arm to the end of his fingers. And apparently what was happening I was told was that he was supposedly moving the poison, or moving the sting, up through the student's body and then out of his fingers, and therefore somehow getting rid of the sting altogether. And the extraordinary thing about this was that it worked, and the moment the sting supposedly left the student's finger he was able to, you know, the pain was gone and he was able to walk, and very often I wouldn't give him a lift back to the school on my motorbike, he'd go and stay and do some shopping and then walk back on his own. So this was somehow or other a far more effective treatment than could be provided by Western medicine at the hospital.

14·4 All the perfumes of Arabia

DOCTOR: I've watched with you for two nights now, but I can't see any truth in what you told me. When was the last time she walked?

GENTLEWOMAN: Since the King went off to war I've seen her get up from her bed, put on a dressing gown, unlock her desk, take out a piece of paper, fold it and write on it. Then she reads it, seals it, and goes back to bed – yet she's fast asleep the whole time.

DOCTOR: There must be something very wrong with her if she's asleep, and yet behaves as if she were awake. Tell me, in this disturbed sleep of hers, as well as walking around and the other things she does, what have you ever heard her say?

GENTLEWOMAN: I'm not telling you that.

DOCTOR: You can tell me – and I think you ought to.

GENTLEWOMAN: I'm not telling you or anyone else, not without a witness to support what I say. Look, here she comes. This is exactly the way she's been before, and, I swear it, fast asleep. Watch her. Keep hidden.

DOCTOR: Where did she get that candle?

GENTLEWOMAN: It was next to her bed. She has a candle there all the time. She insists on it.

DOCTOR: You see her eyes are open.

GENTLEWOMAN: Yes, but she can't see anything.

DOCTOR: What's she doing now? Look at the way she's rubbing her hands together.

GENTLEWOMAN: She often does that. It's as if she's washing her hands. I've known her keep it up for a quarter of an hour.

F Formal and informal

a They say they're sorry but they can't help you any more.
b He was walking down the High Street when he saw two men trying to break into a parked car.
c The dining car's near the back of the train.
d You aren't allowed to drink alcohol in here.
e He say's he's very glad so many people have come to the meeting.

15·1 Memories

1 & 2: See page 78.

3 … And then when I was about 13 my parents were sent abroad to work. They didn't want to disrupt my education and so they sent me off to boarding school. I really hated it there. The food was terrible and we had to go to bed at 9.30 every evening, and we were never allowed to go out in the evening. But of course we did use to sneak out in the evenings, just to go around the village where the school was, and one night I was caught, and I really thought I was going to be expelled, but in fact in the end all that happened was that the headmistress wrote a letter to my parents.

16·1 War and peace

1 Vietcong guerrillas launched a surprise attack on Wednesday on six towns throughout South Vietnam. They also attacked four US air bases, inflicting heavy damage. This is the largest offensive launched by the communist forces so far in the Vietnam War.

2 A force of nearly 3,000 American troops invaded the Caribbean island of Grenada yesterday. Fierce fighting continued today, as Grenadan and Cuban troops resisted the invasion. President Reagan, speaking on television last night, said the troops had been sent to the island to protect Americans living there and to restore democracy.

3 The Tanzanian government has closed its borders to tens of thousands of Rwandan refugees who have fled from their camps in Burundi in fear of their lives. More than 200 refugees are believed to have been killed in a massacre at one of the camps two days ago.

4 The Presidents of Serbia, Bosnia and Croatia yesterday signed a peace treaty which it is hoped will end the 43-month-old war in Bosnia. The agreement was reached after three weeks of intensive negotiations, in which Washington put strong pressure on all three parties to accept the peace plan.

5 Russian troops have now begun to arrive in the town of Kizlyar in Dagestan, where a group of heavily armed Chechen guerrillas are holding around 2,000 hostages in the town's hospital. The hospital is now surrounded by tanks, and a government spokesman has warned the guerrillas that the hostages must not be harmed.

16·4 On the front line

A Most people imagine that being a war correspondent is a pretty dangerous job. Is it in fact as dangerous as that?

B No, it probably looks a lot more dangerous on television or on newspaper than it really is, because you do have a lot of restrictions which actually prevent you from getting to the very dangerous areas. Various sides in a conflict quite often don't actually want a journalist to see exactly what's going on, so they do their best to stop you, especially if you're a foreigner. I myself have only on very few occasions actually got to a front line. Far more often, and this is the case with most journalists I think, you're quite a long way back. So the real dangers are probably of making mistakes. You can accidentally come across a dangerous place, and this is what happened to me in particular. I was driving to Sarajevo, and we found ourselves actually crossing one front line, then in no man's land, where there were dead bodies which hadn't even been reclaimed, because it was so dangerous to be there, and finally crossing over to the other side. At one stage we were surrounded by one of the sides who were actively burning down a village that we happened to be passing through, it was still on fire. So it really is often really by accident that you end up in a dangerous place and it doesn't happen that routinely.

A What about the kind of things you see, I mean, the distress of seeing people wounded and seeing victims, innocent people killed, do you find this affects you emotionally, or can you cut yourself off from it?

B Usually, you're so caught up in your own job, the deadlines that you're involved with, the number of things that you have to do and to cover, that it becomes quite technical, which is actually a help, because that means you can keep your distance, you can insulate yourself emotionally from what's going on. But obviously you can't help but be caught up and I find that even though I've done it so often just driving across miles and miles for hours and hours across areas of Bosnia in which every single village has been burnt, the houses have all been torched deliberately, you know, by one side to stop the people of the other side coming back and living there, that still really affects me, makes me feel very angry and emotional. And obviously on occasions you see people, children especially, when you see children who've been victims of it, I ... The worst occasion was when I saw a group of refugees who'd been driven from their homes quite early on in the war, and there was a young woman who after many hours of walking across a front line carried her baby who'd died and she wouldn't let go. And that, you know, I still remember that, I'll never forget it.

A Being in a war zone and reporting war, you're in a place where important events are happening and life is very exciting. What is it like coming back to London, say, to the ordinary world? Does it seem very flat in comparison?

B Yes, there's always this strange culture shock. It takes a while to get used to the culture shock, you walk round in a daze. And also I'm fortunate, I have a family, so I think that helps. I think if I was living by myself it would be more difficult, it's probably more difficult for journalists who are single. But there is this other thing, I mean, yes, life seems slightly flat and dull, it's an awful thing to say but quite often you miss, when just routine things are going on back home, you miss the adrenalin I suppose and I think there is such a phrase as becoming an 'adrenalin junkie', which I was very aware of. But I think if you're aware of this thing that life is going to seem very flat, then that's at least some precaution.

Reference section

1 Present, past and future

Present tenses

Present simple	works
Present continuous	is working
Present perfect simple	has worked
Present perfect continuous	has been working

• We use these tenses when talking from the standpoint of the present – what things are like *now*.

Present simple
This is used for talking 'in general', or about repeated actions:
– He *comes* from Vladivostok.
– She *works* ten hours a day.

Present continuous
This is used for saying what's happening at the moment or 'around now':
– He can't talk to you now – he's *washing* his hair.
– *Are* you still *going* out with Linda?

Note: Both the Present simple and Present continuous are also used to talk about the *future*. See General grammar reference section, page 126.

Present perfect simple
This is used for talking about recent events, or things which happened in the past when we are interested in their relevance to the present:
– I've *stopped* smoking. (= I don't smoke now)
– I've just *started* a new job. (= now I have a job)

We also use the Present perfect simple to talk about *experience* (things you have done at some time in your life):
– I've *travelled* at lot in East Asia and Australia.
  (= at various times)
– I've never *eaten* raw fish. (= at any time)

Present perfect continuous
This is used for talking about recent activities:
– I've *been working* hard recently.
With *for/since*, it is used to talk about activities which started in the past and are still continuing:
– He's *been working* for 12 hours (and he's still working).

Using Present perfect simple instead of continuous
We use the Present perfect simple instead of the continuous in these cases:
1 with *stative verbs* (see General grammar reference section, page 126):
   – I've *had* a lot to do recently. (*not* ~~been having~~)
   – We've *known* them for years. (*not* ~~been knowing~~)
2 to express *negative* duration (to say how long it is since something happened):
   – I *haven't seen* her for years.
   – She *hasn't played* chess since she was a child.

Past tenses

Past simple	worked
Past continuous	was working
Past perfect	had worked

• We use these tenses when talking about things which are *set in the past*.

Past simple
This is used for talking about events or states in the past, and for telling the main events of a story:
– I *studied* zoology at university.
– Suddenly, I *woke* up.

Past continuous
This is used for saying what was going on (the background to a story):
– The sun *was shining*.
– I *was lying* in my tent when I heard a noise outside.

Past perfect simple
This is used for going back from the past to things that had happened earlier:
– When I arrived, everyone *had* already *finished* eating.
– There *had been* heavy snow the day before.

Future tenses

Future simple	will work
Future continuous	will be working
Future perfect	will have worked

• We use these tenses when talking about things which are *set in the future*.

Future simple
This is used for talking about events or states in the future:
– In the future, people *will live* much longer.
– The film *will finish* at 10 o'clock.

Future continuous
This is used for saying what will be happening at a particular point in the future:
– By 2010, some people *will be living* in space.
– I'll *be waiting* for you when you come out.

Future perfect
This is used for talking about things that will already be complete at a point in the future:
– In ten years' time, we *will have discovered* a cure for cancer.
– By the time I'm 60, I *will have stopped* smoking.

(See also General grammar reference section, page 126.)

Knowledge and experience

- To talk about experience, we can use the Present perfect tense (see above):
  - I've *been* to Los Angeles several times.
  - I've never *used* an IBM computer.

- Other ways to talk about experience:
  - I *have (some) experience of* hotel work.
  - I'm *used to working* with elderly people. (= I've done it before, so I know about it)

- Ways to talk about *knowledge* and *qualifications*:
  - I have *a good knowledge* of Japanese.
  - I'm *familiar with* Macintosh computers.
  - I'm a *trained* mechanic.
  - I'm a *qualified* secretary.
  - I have *qualifications in* Spanish and Italian.

2 Communicating

Types of written and spoken English

message	leave a message (for someone)
note	write a note (to someone), leave a note (for someone)
notes	take/make notes (e.g. from a lecture)
notice	put up a notice
announcement	make an announcement
speech	make/give a speech
lecture	give a lecture
sermon	give a sermon
contract	write/sign a contract
minutes	take the minutes (of a meeting)

- A *note* is usually to ask or remind someone to do something (e.g. 'Please buy more milk. Back at 6'). You *take* or *make notes* from a book or lecture, or to prepare for a speech. *Minutes* are notes you take at a meeting, to record what happened.

- A *notice* gives public information (e.g. 'No smoking', 'Closed until Monday').

- Types of *message*: an email message, a phone message, an answerphone message, a message in a bottle.

Communicating: Idioms

- If you meet someone regularly, or often phone or write to them, you are *in touch with* them. Notice these expressions:

be get keep	in	touch with someone
lose be out of		

In more formal English, we say *be in contact with, lose contact with*, etc. This has the same meaning.

- Other idioms concerned with communicating:
  - *we get on well (with each other)* = we like each other, and have plenty to talk about

  - *we're not on speaking terms* = we don't speak to each other when we meet (because we're enemies)
  - *make small talk* = talk about unimportant things (e.g. the weather)
  - *make it up (with someone)* = become friends again after having an argument

Learning a language

- Learning a language involves:
  - learning *grammar, vocabulary, pronunciation* and *intonation*
  - developing the four *skills: reading, writing, listening* and *speaking*
  - being able to use the language *fluently* (= being able to *communicate* easily) and *accurately* (= not making *mistakes*)

3 Making things clear

Relative clauses

- There are two kinds of relative clause in English:
  - *Defining* (or *identifying*) relative clauses tell us which person or thing the speaker is talking about:
    The people *who live next door* have bought a dog.
    Where's the book *that I lent you*?
  - *Non-defining* (or *non-identifying*) relative clauses just give us more information about the person or thing:
    Mrs Smith, *who lives next door*, has bought a dog.
    I'm reading 'The Idiot', *which is a novel by Dostoyevsky*.
    Non-defining relative clauses are dealt with in Unit 5.

Defining relative clauses: pronouns

	Person	Thing
Subject	who/that	which/that
Object	(who/that)	(which/that)
Possessive	whose	–
Place	–	where

- If the relative pronoun is the object of the relative clause, it can be left out:
  - She's the person you met on Saturday. (= who/that you met)
  - Where's the book I lent you? (= which/that I lent you)

- In more formal English, we use *whom* as an object pronoun to refer to people:
  - He is a man *whom* I admire greatly.

- If the relative clause contains a preposition, it can be left 'hanging' at the end of the clause:
  - Are you the person I spoke *to* yesterday?
  - This is the chair I usually sit *in*.

- In more formal English, the preposition comes before the relative pronoun:
  - Are you the person *to whom* I spoke yesterday?
  - The village *in which* I grew up no longer exists.

Cleft sentences

- We use cleft sentences to give emphasis to a particular part of the sentence. Compare:
  The Americans landed on the Moon, not the Russians.
  → It was the Americans who landed on the Moon, not the Russians, or:
  It wasn't the Russians that landed on the Moon. It was the Americans.
  I admire Peter's *honesty*.
  → The thing I admire about Peter is his honesty.

- Cleft sentences with *It*:

It was John	who spoke to you, (who) you met,	not Alex.
It wasn't Alex	that spoke to you. (that) you met.	It was John.

- Cleft sentences with *What* or *The thing (that)*:

What / The thing	I really enjoy is eating outside.
What / The thing	I hate about Mondays is getting up early.

Participle phrases with *-ing* and *-ed*

- There's a woman. She's sitting on a bench. She's reading a newspaper.
  → There's a woman sitting on a bench reading a newspaper.
- He was lying on the grass. He was stretched out. He had his legs crossed.
  → He was lying stretched out on the grass with his legs crossed.

4 Sports and games

Dangerous sports

- Names of some 'dangerous' sports:

> *In the air:* parachute jumping, skydiving, hang-gliding, ski jumping, bungee jumping
> *On water:* white water rafting/canoeing
> *On land:* mountaineering, rock climbing, off-piste skiing
> *Underground:* potholing
> *Under water:* scuba diving

- People do dangerous sports because they're *exhilarating/thrilling/exciting*. They get a *thrill* out of them.
- You need to be thoroughly *prepared/trained* by a qualified *instructor* or *guide*, and you often need special *equipment* such as *safety helmets*, *ropes* and *axes*.

Sports and games

- Common expressions connected with different sports and games:

Sport/game	Common expressions
tennis, etc.	players, serve, service, hit the ball over the net, in/out, score a point
football, etc.	teams, kick/hit/throw the ball, pass the ball to another player, tackle, score a goal
board games	throw the dice, move a piece, land on a square, take your opponent's piece
card games	shuffle the pack, deal the cards, play a card, win a trick; the four suits: spades, clubs, hearts, diamonds

Issues in sport

- Sportsmen and sportswomen can be either *amateurs* (they play for enjoyment) or *professionals* (they are paid money to take part). In all sports, individuals or teams *compete against* each other, and *matches*, *contests* or *championships* are organised. The winner(s) receive a *prize*, a *medal* or sometimes *prize money*.
- Sometimes *sportsmen* and *sportswomen* (especially *athletes*) take drugs to improve their *performance*. This is illegal, and tests are often carried out before *sports contests*. If the *competitor* is caught, he or she may be *disqualified* or *suspended*.
- *Football matches* attract large numbers of *spectators*. Occasionally there are outbreaks of *violence* between *supporters* (or *fans*) of different *teams*, and so the crowds at major matches are usually tightly *controlled*.

5 Set in the past

Past perfect tenses

- There are two past perfect tenses, Past perfect simple:

I'd / She hadn't	seen the film before.

and Past perfect continuous:

I'd / He'd	been	talking on the phone. / living there for 5 years.

- We use these tenses to *go back* from the past to things that had happened *earlier*.
- We use the Past perfect simple to talk about *previous actions* or *events*:
  – When I returned, the room was empty – everyone *had left*.
  – The restaurant was completely full. Unfortunately, we *hadn't reserved* a table.

- We use the Past perfect continuous to talk about *previous activities*:
  - We were exhausted – we'*d been walking* all day.
  - I was starting to get worried. I'*d been waiting* for over an hour and she still hadn't arrived.
- Past perfect tenses are often used when reporting things people said or thought:
  - He told me his first wife *had died* in a car accident.
  - Later, I discovered that he'*d been lying* to me.

Reporting verbs

Reporting verbs may be followed by several structures:
- verb + *that*
  say   admit   deny
  - He denied that they'd ever met.
  - She admitted that she had lied.
- verb + object + *that*
  tell   remind   warn
  - I reminded him that we had to leave at three.
- verb + *to* + infinitive
  offer   promise   refuse   threaten
  - He offered to lend me his bike. (*not* ~~offered me to~~)
- verb + object + *to* + infinitive
  remind   warn
  - They warned us not to swim out too far.
- verb + *-ing*
  admit   deny   accuse someone of
  - She denied stealing the money.
  - They accused him of accepting bribes.

Non-defining relative clauses

- Non-defining relative clauses are used to give additional information. Compare:
  - My best friend Paula has just moved to Kuusamo.
  - My best friend Paula, *who I went to school with*, has just moved to Kuusamo, *which is a town in the north of Finland*.
  They are always separated from the main part of the sentence by commas.
- In non-defining relative clauses we can use *who*, *which*, *whose* or *where*, but not *that*. It is not possible to leave out the pronoun:
  - My grandmother, *who* is 80 next month, has just gone into hospital.
  - My oldest possession is my camera, *which* I was given for my tenth birthday. (*not* ~~that I was given~~)
  - In 1993 Steven Spielberg made 'Schindler's List', *for which* he received an Oscar.
  - The shop at the end of the street, *where* I usually buy my bread, has closed down.
- In more formal English, we can use *whom* as an object pronoun or after prepositions:
  - Professor Johnson, *whom* you may already know, will talk to us about butterflies.
  - Her brother, *to whom* she dedicated her first novel, is still alive.

(See also Defining relative clauses, Unit 3.)

Sequence expressions

- Structures that emphasise that there was a *short interval* between two events:

As soon as The moment	I saw the car, I decided to buy it.

(= I saw the car. Immediately, I decided to buy it.)

- Structures that emphasise that there was a *long interval* between two events:

It was only when It wasn't until	I saw his house that I realised that he was poor.

(= At first I thought he was rich. After some time, I saw his house. Then I realised he was poor.)

6 Do it yourself

Instructions

- Some common expressions found in instructions:
  - Add boiling water.
  - Rinse thoroughly.
  - Apply two coats of paint.
  - Select the desired programme.
  - Wait until surfaces are completely dry.
  - Stir well.
  - Ensure (that) surfaces are free from dirt.
  - Leave to dry overnight.
  - Press the button marked 'Play'.
- Articles and pronouns are often omitted in instructions:
  - Apply paint and leave to dry = Apply *the* paint and leave *it* to dry.
- Notice that instructions often use special verbs:

Instructions	'Normal' English
ensure that	make sure that
apply	put on
insert	put in
position together	put together
depress	press down

Problems and repairs

- Common household problems:
  - The glass is *cracked/broken*.
  - My dress is *torn*.
  - The door's *rotten*.
  - The paint is *peeling (off)*.
  - The pipe is *leaking*.
  - The walls are *damp*.
  - There's a *stain* on the carpet.
  - The tyre has got a *puncture*.
  - My coat has got a button *missing*.

- Some of these words can be used as verbs or nouns:

It's cracked.	There's a crack in it.
It's torn.	There's a tear (/teər/) in it.
It's leaking.	There's a leak in it.
It's stained.	There's a stain on it.

- 'Mending' verbs:

mend	(re)paint
repair	stick (on/together)
replace	sew (up/on)

- Notice the structure *needs + -ing*:

The door needs	mending. repainting. replacing.

Cooking

- 'Cooking' verbs:

boil	fry	bake
simmer	grill	roast

- To *simmer* is to boil very gently.
- You *bake* bread or cakes in the oven; you *roast* meat in the oven.
- To *cook* is a general word: 'cooked food' means 'not raw' (it could be boiled, baked or fried).

- Other verbs used for preparing food:

chop	mix	melt	pour
slice	add	sprinkle	serve
peel	stir		

You *mix* two or more things together:
- *Mix* the eggs with the flour.
- *Mix* the eggs and the flour together.

You *stir* things round (usually with a spoon):
- *Stir* the sauce slowly.

You *pour* liquids:
- *Pour* the sauce over the fish.

You *sprinkle* sugar, grated cheese, breadcrumbs, etc.:
- *Sprinkle* sugar over the top of the cake.

7 Working it out

must, might and can't

- The model verbs *must*, *might* and *can't* are used for drawing conclusions or making deductions:

  They must be at home = I'm sure they are at home
  They might be at home = Perhaps they're at home
  They can't be at home = I'm sure they're not at home

- Like other modal verbs, *must*, *might* and *can't* are followed by the infinitive without *to*. There are four possible forms:

	Simple	Continuous
Present	work	be working
Past	have worked	have been working

  - He *must work* hard – he looks worn out all the time. (= in general, every day)
  - They *can't be working* – there's no light on in the office. (= at the moment)
  - She *must have worked* hard in her life. (= in the past)
  - They *can't have been working* – there was no light on in the office. (= when I went there)

- *Must*, *might* and *can't* can also be followed by a passive infinitive:
  - It *can't be made* of silk – it's not shiny enough.
  - This picture *might have been taken* during the War.

'Unreal' conditionals

- We use *if + Past tense* (2nd conditional) to imagine unreal things in the *present*:
  - If they weren't at home, the door would be locked.

- We use *if + Past perfect tense* (3rd conditional) to imagine unreal things in the *past*:
  - If they'd seen us, they would have waved.

- We can also mix the two types of conditional in one sentence. One part can refer to the present, and one part to the past:
  - If they weren't at home, they would have locked the door.
  - If you'd broken your leg, you wouldn't be able to walk.

- Notice how we can combine *must*, *might* and *can't* with conditional sentences:
  - They must be at home – otherwise the door would be locked.
  - You can't have broken your leg. If you had, you wouldn't be able to walk.

Appearance

'Sense' verbs

look sound smell taste feel	+ adjective like + noun as if + clause

– He *looks* rather young.
– It doesn't *feel like* leather.
– It *sounds as if* there's someone at the door.

• In informal English, people often use *looks like*, etc. before a clause, instead of *as if*: You look like you need a rest; It sounds like there's someone at the door.

General impression: seem *and* appear

He	seems appears	to like classical music to be living alone to have been in the army

• *Seem* is normally followed by *to* + infinitive, but can also be followed by an *adjective*, by a *noun* or by *like* + *noun*:
   – She seems to be rather sad *or* She seems rather sad.
   – They seem to be interesting people *or* They seem (like) interesting people.

Reason and purpose

• We talk about the *reason why/that* people do things:
   – There are various reasons why people keep dogs.
   – One reason that people keep dogs is for protection.

• We can often leave out *why* and *that*:
   – The main reason I went there was to see a friend.
   – One reason people keep dogs is for protection.

• We talk about doing things *for a reason*:
   – People keep dogs for various reasons.
   – I went there for the same reason that you did.

• Structures expressing purpose:

Many people smoke	*to* relax. *in order to* relax. *so as to* relax. *as a way of* relax*ing*.

8 In the market-place

Careers

• General areas and typical jobs:

business	sales manager, accountant
arts	sculptor, actor, designer
entertainment	comedian, singer
education	lecturer, educational adviser
health	nurse, surgeon, hospital manager
welfare	social worker, welfare officer
media	TV presenter, journalist
industry	factory worker, manager
agriculture	farmer, forestry worker
technology	researcher, engineer
the environment	architect, ecologist
politics	politician, MP, minister
service industries	travel agent, salesperson

• The person in charge of a *company* or *organisation* is the *manager* (in informal English, the *boss*). People who are *employed* in the company are *employees*.

If you work for yourself, you are *self-employed*.

People who work in offices are often called *white-collar workers*. People who work with their hands are *manual workers*.

• Talking about ability and skill:
   – She's *good at* communicating with people / making money / designing things.
   – He's *good with* figures / his hands / children.
   – He's *a good* listener/communicator.
   – She's got *a good* business *sense* / artistic *sense* / *sense of* design.

• Things you might be interested in when applying for a job:
   – opportunities for promotion / for travel / to meet people
   – pay, working conditions, working hours, holidays.

Companies

• Expressions for talking about companies and business:
   – She *runs* a small business/company; he *works for* a computer company; we're *setting up* / *starting* a new business; the company is *launching* a new *product*.
   – They *broke even* (= covered their costs) / *made a profit* / *made a loss* / *went bankrupt*.
   – The company *has a turnover of* £100,000 a year (= the total amount of money it takes in).
   – They *took out a bank loan* (= borrowed money from the bank); they *paid off* the loan; they had to *pay* 5% *interest on* the loan.
   – They *took on* (= employed) more *staff*; they had to *lay staff off* (= ask them to leave); several employees *were made redundant* (= lost their jobs).

Advertising

• Some adjectives to describe advertisements:

appealing	shocking
eye-catching	offensive
persuasive	misleading

• In most countries, there are *rules* or *guidelines* about advertising. If an advertisement breaks these rules, the advertiser may be asked to *withdraw* the advertisement, or it may be *banned*.

9 Possibilities

will and would

• *will* is used for *making predictions*, and for saying what you expect (or don't expect) to happen:
  – I expect it *will* rain tomorrow.
  – Do you think there *will* be another world war in our lifetime?
  – He's taking his driving test tomorrow, but somehow I don't think he'*ll* pass it.

• *would* is used for *imagining* things which you don't see as really going to happen:
  – What *would* you do if you met a polar bear?
  – Why don't you give up smoking? That *would* make your cough better.

• Notice how, in the same context, we can change from *will* (for predicting what will happen) to *would* (for imagining other possibilities):
  – The council's plan to widen the main road *won't* solve the traffic problem – it *will* just encourage more people to use their cars. A better idea *would* be to make the road narrower, then people *would* leave their cars at home and use public transport.

depend on

• *depend on* can be followed by a noun or an indirect question:
  – How long will it take to get there?

It depends on	the traffic.
	how much traffic there is.
	whether we get stuck in a traffic jam.

• Before indirect questions, we can also use *it depends* without *on*:
  – It depends how much traffic there is.
  – It depends whether we get stuck in a traffic jam.

• Notice the expression *It depends*:
  – How long will it take to get there?
  – It depends. (= It depends on various things)

Expressing probability

Two ways of expressing probability:
will/won't + adverb

They	will certainly will probably probably won't certainly won't	reply to your letter.

is certain/likely/unlikely to

They	are certain are likely are unlikely are certain not	to reply to your letter.

• Notice that *likely* and *unlikely* are *adjectives*, so we say:
  – He'*s likely to* come today.
  – There *are unlikely to* be many people there.

• In US English *likely* can also be used as an adverb:
  – He *will likely* come today.

• *likely* and *unlikely* can also be used regularly as adjectives:
  – She might phone, but it doesn't seem very *likely*.
  – I think the whole story sounds extremely *unlikely*.

Alternatives

• Expressions for weighing up alternatives:

Either … or …
Alternatively …
…, or else …
Another possibility …

  – *Either* you could go straight to university, *or* you could wait for a year and earn some money first.
  – You could go straight to university, *or else* you could wait for a year and earn some money first.
  – You could go straight to university. *Alternatively*, you could wait for a year and earn some money first.
  – You could go straight to university. *Another possibility would be to* wait for a year and earn some money first.

10 Life, the universe and everything

Branches of science

- Sciences and scientists:

science	scientist
chemistry	chemist
physics	physicist
mathematics	mathematician
biology	biologist
genetics	geneticist
astronomy	astronomer
zoology	zoologist
geology	geologist

- Some basic scientific ideas:
  - The main *gases* in the air are *oxygen, nitrogen* and *carbon dioxide*. Water consists of two *elements*: *oxygen* and *hydrogen*.
  - *Atoms* combine together to form *molecules*.
  - According to Darwin's theory of *evolution*, different *species* of plants and animals have *evolved* over millions of years by natural selection.
  - When the *surface* of the Earth moves suddenly, it causes *earthquakes*.
  - The Earth and the other *planets* in the *solar system revolve* round the Sun. Our solar system is part of the *galaxy* we call the Milky Way.
  - The main groups of *vertebrates* (animals with backbones) are fish, *reptiles*, *amphibians*, birds and *mammals*. Many *species* of animals (such as dinosaurs) have become *extinct*.
  - Many *diseases* are caused by *bacteria* or by *viruses*. Diseases caused by bacteria can often be *treated* with *antibiotics*.
  - A *triangle* has three *corners* (or angles) and three *sides*. Some other common *geometrical shapes* are: *square*, *rectangle* and *circle*.

The environment

- Environmental issues:
  - *Nuclear power stations* use *radioactive* materials, and produce *radioactive waste*. If there is an accident, *radioactivity* can escape into the atmosphere.
  - Gases, such as car *exhaust fumes* and smoke from *power stations*, cause *atmospheric pollution*. They also prevent heat escaping from the Earth's atmosphere, and this causes the '*greenhouse effect*'. It is believed that the greenhouse effect contributes to *global warming*.
  - In modern farming, *crops* are *sprayed* with *chemicals* and *pesticides*. Some people believe that these are *harmful* to people and may cause *cancer*.
  - Because of the destruction of their *habitats* (especially *tropical rain forests*) many species of animals and plants are becoming *extinct*.

'Unscientific' beliefs

Beliefs	What people believe
astrology	The star sign you were born under affects your character.
telepathy	People can communicate directly by thinking.
psychokinesis	People can move objects by concentrating their thoughts on them.
fortune-telling	People can tell the future from cards, coffee cups, etc.
witchcraft	People can influence other people by casting a magic spell.
reincarnation	After they die, people are reborn in another body.
superstition	Particular things (e.g. black cats) bring good or bad luck.
ghosts	Ghosts of dead people sometimes appear in the place where they died.

11 Evaluating

Time comparison

Cities	are noisier than aren't as pleasant as	they used to be.
Most people	have more free time than don't work as hard as	they used to.

- Notice that the verb *be* is repeated after *used to*, but other verbs are omitted:
  - He*'s* healthier than he used to *be*.
  - He *looks* healthier than he used to. (*not* ~~used to look~~)
- We can also make comparisons beginning with *used to*:
  - Cities *used not to* be as noisy as *they are now*.
  - Most people *used to* work harder than *they do now*.
- We can also use the Present perfect:
  - Cities *have become* noisier (over the last 50 years).
  - People *have started* having more free time.

Evaluation structures

It's a good idea It's not a good idea	to go on a diet.

It's worth(while) It's not worth There's no point in	going on a diet.

- *It's not worth doing* and *There's no point in doing* both mean that you can do something, but it will achieve nothing:
  - There's *no point in* giving her flowers – she wouldn't notice them.
  - It's *not worth* taking a taxi – you can walk there in five minutes.

- We can say something is *worth doing* or is *worthwhile doing*:
  - It's really *worth*(*while*) visit*ing* Scotland – it's a beautiful country.
- Notice these expressions with *worth* and *worthwhile*:

I'm glad I saw that film.	It was really worth it. It was really worthwhile.

Causative verbs

enable allow force encourage help make it easier for	someone	to + infinitive

stop prevent discourage save	someone	from + -ing

Examples

- Fax machines *enable* people *to* send letters instantly.
- The mist *prevented* us *from* see*ing* clearly.
- Having a job in a factory *forced* him *to* get up early.
- Dishwashers *save* you (*from*) wash*ing* all the dishes by hand.
- The new tax laws *will encourage* people *to* save money.
- They increased parking charges to *discourage* people *from* driv*ing* into the city centre.

Advantages and disadvantages

One The Another (etc.)	advantage of disadvantage of drawback of problem with trouble with (good) thing about	......	is ...

- All these expressions are followed by a noun or an *-ing* form:

One advantage of	old age being old	is that you have lots of time.

- They are used to 'label' what you are talking about as good, bad, difficult, interesting, etc. Compare:

  If you live in the country, it isn't easy to go shopping.
  → *One of the main disadvantages of* living in the country *is that* it isn't easy to go shopping.
  When you're abroad, everything seems slightly unusual.
  → *The most exciting thing about* being abroad *is that* everything seems slightly unusual.

12 Yourself and others

Character adjectives

cheerful	sociable	cautious	vain
optimistic	talkative	fussy	self-centred
light-hearted	inquisitive	sensitive	aggressive
carefree	nosy	insecure	determined

- The following adjectives have a negative meaning:
  talkative = you talk too much
  nosy = you want to know other people's business
  fussy = you worry about every detail
  insecure = you're unsure of yourself
  vain = you admire yourself
  aggressive = you tend to quarrel or fight with people
- *sensitive* can have a positive or a negative meaning:
  - He's a very *sensitive* person who appreciates beauty. (= with fine feelings)
  - Don't be so *sensitive* – I was only joking. (= easily hurt)
  In the negative sense, we can also say *over-sensitive*:
  - Now he won't speak to me – I think he's being a bit *over-sensitive*.
  Notice the word *sensible*, which has quite a different meaning = 'having good sense':
  - She was *sensible* enough not to carry too much money around with her.
- Compare:
  - *self-centred* (negative) = always thinking about yourself and putting yourself first
  - *self-confident* (usually positive) = sure of yourself
  - *self-satisfied* (negative) = too pleased with yourself
- Notice how we use the expressions *tend to* and *have a tendency to* in describing what people are like:
  - She's very sociable, but she *tends to* be rather nosy.
  - He *has a tendency to* worry too much about details.

Relationships

- Some things that people often look for in a relationship with a partner:

honesty	respect for the other person
friendship	ability to communicate
equality	sense of humour
good looks	shared interests

- Other kinds of relationship:
  - *colleagues* (people you work with)
  - *neighbours* (people who live near you)
  - *acquaintances* (people you know but are not very close to)
- You may:
  - know other people well or just know them *by sight*
  - *get acquainted with* or *make friends with* them
  - *get on well* or *badly with* them
  - have *a lot*, *not much* or *nothing in common with* them
  - *envy* them (or *feel envious of* them) (= you wish you had what they have).

13 Right and wrong

should(n't) have

He	should shouldn't	have + -ed

She	should shouldn't	have been + -ing

- We use *should(n't) have + -ed* for criticising things people *did* or *didn't do*:
  - She should have stopped at the traffic lights (but she didn't).
  - You shouldn't have shouted at him (but you did).
- We use *should(n't) have been + -ing* for criticising things people *were* or *weren't doing*:
  - She shouldn't have been driving so fast. (that's why she couldn't stop)
  - You should have been paying attention. (then you would have heard what I said)
- Other expressions for talking about right and wrong:
  - She was (quite) *right/wrong to* complain about it.
  - People *have a right to* say what they think.
  - The government *has no right to* imprison people without trial.
  - It was *your own fault (that)* you ran out of money – you should have taken more with you.
  - I wasn't *to blame for* the accident – I wasn't even there.

needn't have & could have

He	needn't could	have + -ed

- *needn't have (done)* is used to talk about what someone did that *wasn't necessary*:
  - They *needn't have brought* food to the party (= they brought some food but there was plenty already).
  - I *needn't have got* here on time (= I got here on time, but then I had to wait for everyone else).
- *could have (done)* is used to talk about an *opportunity* to do something, but the person didn't do it:
  - Why did you hire a car? You *could have borrowed* mine.
  - I didn't know you were staying here. We *could have met* for a drink.
- Notice that *needn't have done* and *could have done* can often be used in the same context:
  - You *needn't have hired* a car – you *could have borrowed* mine.
  - I *needn't have got up* early this morning – I *could have stayed* in bed for another hour.

might have & could have

You	might could	have + -ed

- *Might/could have (done)* is used to criticise people for what they *didn't* do. It is milder and less direct than *should have (done)*:
  - You *might/could have told* me you'd be late. (you didn't tell me)
- *Might/could have (done)* is also used in a different sense: to imagine things that didn't in fact happen:
  - He was crazy to go swimming in this weather: he *might/could have drowned*. (luckily, he didn't drown)
- *Might (as well) have (done)* is also used to say that it *wasn't worth* doing something:
  - It wasn't worth taking a taxi – we *might as well have walked*.

Contrasting ideas

- Some common ways of contrasting two ideas:

Mild contrast

It may be true that … To some extent it's true that …	But also … On the other hand, …

Moderate contrast

Many people think that … People often claim that … It's commonly believed that …	But in fact, … However, … In fact, however, …

Strong contrast

Many people think that … People often claim that …	On the contrary, … In fact, …

- *It may be true that* supermarkets make shopping easier. *On the other hand*, they make it very difficult for smaller shops to survive.
- *Many people think that* the United Nations has achieved almost nothing at all. *In fact, however*, just providing a place where different nations can talk to each other is itself a sign of progress.
- *It simply isn't true* that the government is helping poor people. *On the contrary*, their policies are making poor people even poorer.

14 Body and mind

Diseases

- Many diseases are *infectious* (you can catch them from the air, from flies, water, etc.).
  Some diseases are *curable* (= you can cure them), some are *incurable* (= you cannot cure them) or *fatal* (= you die from them).
  An *outbreak* of cholera = many people get it at the same time. A cholera *epidemic* = a very large number of people get it at the same time.
  The *symptoms* of 'flu are a high temperature and aching limbs.

Medical treatment

- Verbs and nouns connected with medical treatment:

Verbs	Nouns
examine	examination
operate	operation
prescribe	prescription
vaccinate	vaccination
inoculate	inoculation
X-ray	X-ray

- If you go to see a doctor, he/she will probably examine you (give you an *examination*). He/She may *prescribe* medicine for you to take (write/give you a *prescription*).

- If you need an *operation*, you *go into hospital*. They will give you an *anaesthetic*, and the operation will be performed by a *surgeon* (he/she will *operate* on you).

- You can be *vaccinated* (or *inoculated*) to protect you against catching certain diseases (e.g. cholera, measles, polio). Babies usually have their first *vaccination* (or *inoculation*) at the age of six months. In everyday conversation, people talk about *having an injection*.

- If you have a *toothache*, you should go to a dentist. He/She will examine your teeth, and may give you a filling.

- You can take your *temperature* by putting a *thermometer* under your tongue. If your temperature is more than 35°, we say 'You've got a temperature' or 'You've got a fever'.

- If you think you've broken your leg, you can have it *X-rayed* at the hospital.

- If you cut your finger, you put a *plaster* on it. If you cut your hand badly (or if you sprain your wrist), you may have to put a *bandage* round it.

Alternative medicine

- Some forms of alternative medicine and healing:

Type	What they use
traditional medicine	herbs and traditional remedies
homeopathy	homeopathic medicines
acupuncture	needles
faith healing	religious faith and touch

15   Using the passive

The passive

Active	Someone *stole* his wallet.
	Terrorists *have kidnapped* them.
Passive	His wallet *was stolen*.
	They*'ve been kidnapped* by terrorists.

- In forming the passive, the object of the active sentence (*wallet, them*) becomes the *subject* of the passive sentence.

- The passive is formed with *be + past participle*. It can be in any tense: past, present or future.

	Simple	Continuous
Present	is built	is being built
Present perfect	has been built	–
Past	was built	was being built
Past perfect	had been built	–
Future	will be built	–
Present infinitive	be built	–
Past infinitive	have been built	–
-ing form	being built	–

- These days, most houses *are built* of concrete.
- Their house isn't finished yet. It's still *being built*.
- This is where the new airport *will be built*.
- In my opinion, the school shouldn't *have been built* so near the main road.

Notice that the continuous form is normally only used in the present and past tenses.

Using the passive

- We often use the passive when we are interested in *what happened* rather than in who did the action:
  - His wallet *was stolen*. (we don't know who stole it)
  - She's just *been given* a new job. (obviously, by her employers)
  - The airport *will be finished* next spring. (it isn't important who finishes it)

- We also use the passive in order to keep *the same subject* over several sentences:
  - I had a terrible time crossing the border. First I had to wait for two hours, and then I *was interrogated* for an hour by the secret police. (I'm talking about *my experiences*, so I want to keep *I* as the subject)

- Notice that the passive is especially common in scientific writing, especially in describing processes:
  - First the metal *is heated* to a temperature of 500°, then it *is poured* into a large container.

The passive with 'get'

- In conversational English, we often use the passive with *get* instead of *be*, especially with particular verbs describing accidental events, e.g.:

get lost	get killed	get stolen
get stuck	get mugged	get caught

- Take a map, in case you *get lost*.
- He tried to cheat the tax office, but he *got caught*.

- The passive is also commonly used with *get* to talk about things that happen *often* or *repeatedly*:
  - She often *gets invited* to read her poetry, but she doesn't always *get paid*.

The 'have' passive

Active	They're repairing her car.
Passive	Her car is being repaired.
'Have' passive	She's *having* her car *repaired*.
Active	Someone stole my bike.
Passive	My bike was stolen.
'Have' passive	I *had* my bike *stolen*.

- The 'have' passive is formed with *have* (+ object) + *past participle*. Like the normal passive, it can be in any tense:
  - *Present simple*: I usually *have* my hair *cut* on Saturday.
  - *going to*: He's going to *have* his eyes *tested*.
  - *Present perfect*: Help! I've just *had* my handbag *snatched*!
  - *Past continuous*: When I walked in, he *was having* his back *massaged*.
  - *-ing form*: I hate *having* my photograph *taken*.
- The 'have' passive can be used:
  - for things that you *arrange to happen* (have your eyes tested, have your photograph taken, have your house painted)
  - for things that *happen to you without you intending them* (have your face slapped, have your car stolen, have your house broken into)
- Notice the difference between the *'have' passive* and the *Present perfect tense*:
  - I've cut my hair (Present perfect = I've done it myself)
  - I usually *have* my hair *cut* at Toni's ('have' passive, = I usually get them to do it)

Passive reporting verbs

He is They are	known believed said thought assumed reported	to	work for the Mafia. be living in Chicago. have robbed a bank.

- *He is thought to be* … means the same as *People think he is* … Compare:

> *People think* he works for the Mafia.
> *It is thought that* he works for the Mafia.
> *He is thought to* work for the Mafia.

- Passive reporting verbs are especially common in more formal written English (e.g. newspaper reports). In conversational English, active forms are more usual:
  - They say he robbed a bank.
  - Everyone knows he's living in Chicago.

16 World affairs

War and peace

- Some common verb/noun pairs:

Verb	Noun
attack	attack
fight	fighting
invade	invasion
resist	resistance
damage	damage
negotiate	negotiations
agree	agreement

- Examples:
  - Rebel troops *attacked* the capital.
  - Rebel troops *launched an attack on* the capital.
  - The two sides *fought* through the night.
  - *Fighting* continued through the night.
  - American forces *invaded* the island.
  - Local troops *resisted* the *invasion*.
  - Local troops *put up* fierce *resistance to* the invasion.
  - They *damaged* several buildings.
  - They *caused* severe *damage to* several buildings.
  - After *negotiating* for a long time, the two sides *reached agreement*.
  - After long *negotiations*, the two sides *agreed* to end the war.
- Other expressions:
  - *Refugees fled* (past of *flee*) across the border. They found shelter in *refugee camps*.
  - The rebels *took* several *hostages* and held them in a hospital building. Troops *surrounded* the building. After negotiations the rebels agreed to *free* the hostages.
  - The two sides *signed* a *peace treaty* (or *peace agreement*) to end the war.

Political systems

- In a *democracy*, people vote in a *general election*. The *party* that wins forms the *government*. The other parties are *opposition* parties. The leader of the government is the *prime minister* or *president*, and he/she chooses other *ministers* to form the *cabinet*.
- In a *monarchy* (e.g. Britain, Sweden, Thailand), the highest person is the *monarch* (king or queen). In a *republic* (e.g. Russia, the USA, South Africa), the head of state is the *president*.
- Areas of government:

Area	Concerned with
health	hospitals, doctors, health care
education	schools, universities, adult education
defence	army, navy, air force, weapons
economic affairs	the economy, taxation
foreign affairs	relations with other countries
home affairs	police, prisons, housing
employment	jobs, unemployment
transport	roads, public transport
environment	pollution, wildlife
agriculture	farming, forestry

General grammar reference: the English tense system

- There are three 'time frames' in the English tense system: the present, the past and the future. Within each time frame, there are four 'aspects': *simple, continuous, perfect simple* and *perfect continuous*. This gives the twelve main tenses of English.

	Simple	Continuous
Present Present perfect	works has worked	is working has been working
Past Past perfect	worked had worked	was working had been working
Future Future perfect	will work will have worked	will be working will have been working

Simple tenses

- The Present simple is used to talk about things in general, or repeated actions:
  - My sister *speaks* fluent Arabic.
  - I *have* a sauna every Friday evening.
- The Past simple is used to talk about actions or states in the past:
  - They *got* married last Saturday.
  - In the Middle Ages, forests *covered* most of Europe.
- The Future simple is used to talk about events or states in the future:
  - The world *will end* in 2050.
  - *Will* you still *be* here this evening?

Continuous tenses

- Continuous tenses are used to talk about activities *going on* at a particular moment:
  Present: He's *staying* with friends at the moment.
  Wait a minute – I'm just *changing*.
  Past: When I came in, they *were playing* cards.
  Future: By next spring, we'll *be living* in Canada.
  I'll *be waiting* outside (when you arrive).

Perfect tenses

- Perfect simple tenses are used to talk about actions that are *already finished* or *complete* at a particular moment (when they happened is not important, but rather the fact that they are complete):
  Present: She's *been* all over the world. (= she knows a lot of countries)
  I've *changed* my clothes. (= now I'm wearing new ones)
  Past: When I came in, they *had* already *left*. (= they weren't there any more)
  Future: By next spring, we'll *have moved* to Canada. (= we'll be there by then)
- Perfect continuous tenses are used to talk about *activities* going on *just before* or *up to* a particular moment:
  Present: I've *been washing* the car. (that's why I'm wet)
  We've *been living* together for a year now.

Past: They'd *been waiting* for over an hour, and they were starting to get impatient.
Future: By next Sunday, I'll *have been working* here for a year.

Stative verbs

- Some verbs are normally used only with simple tenses. There are four main types:
  - *verbs expressing attitudes*: like, love, hate, prefer, want, wish, need
  - *verbs of knowledge and belief*: know, believe, doubt, mean, remember, forget, understand, think (= believe)
  - *verbs connected with having and being*: be, have (= possess), own, belong to, include, consist of, seem
  - *verbs of the senses*: see, hear, sound, taste, smell (= give out a smell)
- Examples:
  - This cake *tastes* wonderful. (*not* is tasting)
  - We've *known* each other for years. (*not* been knowing)
  - He desperately *needed* help. (*not* was needing)

Talking about the future

- We can talk about the future in various ways in English:
  will
  We use *will* to make predictions:
  - I expect a lot of people *will* come to the lecture.
  - Don't leave the butter out in the sun – it *will* melt.

  We also use *will* when *making a decision* to do something:
  - I think I'll have an ice-cream.
  - I know. I'll ask Mary what to do.

  Present simple
  We use the present simple to talk about future events which are part of a *programme* or *timetable*:
  - My train *gets* in at 6.30 this evening.
  - Don't be late: the concert *starts* at 8 o'clock.

  Present continuous
  We use the present continuous to talk about things that are *already arranged* for the future:
  - We're *having* a party on Friday: do you want to come?
  - I'm *playing* table tennis this evening.

  going to
  We use *going to*:
  1 to express *intention*:
    - When I grow up, I'm *going* to be an airline pilot.
    - I'm *going* to have a hot bath and go to bed early.
  2 to talk about things that have *already started to happen*:
    - Look out! We're *going* to crash! (we've already started skidding)
    - She's *going* to have a baby. (she's pregnant)

  Note: We do not use *will* to express intention, so we wouldn't say 'I'll have a hot bath' unless we are *actually deciding* to do that as we speak.

Irregular verbs

Infinitive	Simple past	Past participle
be	was/were	been
beat	beat	beaten
become	became	become
begin	began	begun
bend	bent	bent
bite	bit	bitten
blow	blew	blown
break	broke	broken
bring	brought	brought
burn	burnt	burnt
build	built	built
buy	bought	bought
can	could	(been able)
catch	caught	caught
choose	chose	chosen
come	came	come
cost	cost	cost
cut	cut	cut
do	did	done
draw	drew	drawn
dream	dreamt	dreamt
drink	drank	drunk
drive	drove	driven
eat	ate	eaten
fall	fell	fallen
feed	fed	fed
feel	felt	felt
fight	fought	fought
find	found	found
fly	flew	flown
forget	forgot	forgotten
forgive	forgave	forgiven
freeze	froze	frozen
get	got	got
give	gave	given
go	went	gone (been)
grow	grew	grown
hang	hung	hung
have	had	had
hear	heard	heard
hide	hid	hidden
hit	hit	hit
hold	held	held
hurt	hurt	hurt
keep	kept	kept
know	knew	known
lay	laid	laid
lead	led	led
learn	learnt	learnt
leave	left	left
lend	lent	lent
let	let	let
lie	lay	lain
lose	lost	lost
make	made	made
mean	meant	meant
meet	met	met
pay	paid	paid
put	put	put
read	read	read
ride	rode	ridden
ring	rang	rung
rise	rose	risen
run	ran	run
say	said	said
see	saw	seen
sell	sold	sold
send	sent	sent
set	set	set

Infinitive	Simple past	Past participle
shake	shook	shaken
shine	shone	shone
shoot	shot	shot
show	showed	shown
shut	shut	shut
sing	sang	sung
sink	sank	sunk
sit	sat	sat
sleep	slept	slept
smell	smelt	smelt
speak	spoke	spoken
spell	spelt	spelt
spend	spent	spent
spread	spread	spread
stand	stood	stood
steal	stole	stolen
sweep	swept	swept
swim	swam	swum
swing	swung	swung
take	took	taken
teach	taught	taught
tear	tore	torn
tell	told	told
think	thought	thought
throw	threw	thrown
understand	understood	understood
wake	woke	woken
wear	wore	worn
win	won	won
write	wrote	written

Phonetic symbols

Vowels

Symbol	Example
/iː/	tree /triː/
/i/	many /ˈmeni/
/ɪ/	sit /sɪt/
/e/	bed /bed/
/æ/	back /bæk/
/ʌ/	sun /sʌn/
/ɑː/	car /kɑː/
/ɒ/	hot /hɒt/
/ɔː/	horse /hɔːs/
/ʊ/	full /fʊl/
/uː/	moon /muːn/
/ɜː/	girl /gɜːl/
/ə/	arrive /əˈraɪv/
	water /ˈwɔːtə/
/eɪ/	late /leɪt/
/aɪ/	time /taɪm/
/ɔɪ/	boy /bɔɪ/
/əʊ/	home /həʊm/
/aʊ/	out /aʊt/
/ɪə/	hear /hɪə/
/eə/	there /ðeə/
/ʊə/	pure /pjʊə/

Consonants

Symbol	Example
/p/	pull /pʊl/
/b/	bad /bæd/
/t/	take /teɪk/
/d/	dog /dɒg/
/k/	cat /kæt/
/g/	go /gəʊ/
/tʃ/	church /tʃɜːtʃ/
/dʒ/	age /eɪdʒ/
/f/	for /fɔː/
/v/	love /lʌv/
/θ/	thick /θɪk/
/ð/	this /ðɪs/
/s/	sit /sɪt/
/z/	zoo /zuː/
/ʃ/	shop /ʃɒp/
/ʒ/	leisure /ˈleʒə/
/h/	house /haʊs/
/m/	make /meɪk/
/n/	name /neɪm/
/ŋ/	bring /brɪŋ/
/l/	look /lʊk/
/r/	road /rəʊd/
/j/	young /jʌŋ/
/w/	wear /weə/

Stress

We show stress by a mark (/ˈ/) before the stressed syllable:
later /ˈleɪtə; arrive /əˈraɪv/; information /ɪnfəˈmeɪʃn/.

Acknowledgements

The authors would like to thank the following for their contributions to *Language in Use* Upper-intermediate:

- for contributing to the listening and reading material: Colin Aitkin, Anginette Barton, Fran Brooks, Nick Brooks, Mark Calland, Sean Connolly, Dawn Coutts, Bryan Cruden, Shiroma da Silva, Mary Drummond, Hazel Jones, Thomas Jones, Anastasia Katsikiotis, Richard Keyworth, Meredith Levy, Steve Mitchell, Stephen Myers, Philip Older, Louisa Preskett, Paula Preskett, Gaby Rado, Paul Roberts, Philippe Roy, Simon Taylor, Diana Thompson, Pam Thompson, Ingrid Williams, Jan Williams, Larissa Williams, Gabriella Zaharias; staff and students of Abon Language School, Bristol, and BPELF, Edinburgh; and all the actors whose voices were recorded in studio sessions.
- for advice and help with the pronunciation exercises: Martin Hewings of The University of Birmingham.
- for designing the course: James Arnold (Gecko Ltd).
- for commissioning artwork: Wendy Homer (Gecko Ltd).
- for the production of the recorded material: Martin Williamson (Prolingua Productions) and Peter and Diana Thompson (Studio AVP).
- for photography: Chris Coggins.
- for picture research: Sandie Huskinson-Rolfe of PHOTOSEEKERS.
- for clearance of permissions: Sophie Dukan.

The authors would also like to thank the following at Cambridge University Press:

- Colin Hayes, for his continuing support and help.
- Peter Donovan for organising the project.
- Joanne Currie for overseeing the design of the course.
- Linda Matthews for control of production.
- Sue Wiseman and Val Grove for general administrative help.

Special thanks go to:

- James Dingle of Cambridge University Press, for his expert management of the various stages of the project, and for his continuing commitment to *Language in Use*.
- Meredith Levy, our Editor, for her professionalism, good judgement and tireless attention to detail.

The authors and publishers would like to thank the following individuals for their help in commenting on the material and for the invaluable feedback which they provided:

Silvia Ronchetti, Buenos Aires, Argentina; Julia Barraco, British Council, Athens, Greece; Richard Rice, Associazione Culturale Delle Lingue Europee, Bologna, Italy; Niall Henderson, Chiuro, Italy; John Eaglesham, British School of Milan, Italy; Jonathan Wright, The Language Project, Bristol, UK; Matthew Wicks, Language Studies International, Cambridge, UK; Brian Cruden, Basil Paterson Edinburgh Langauge Foundation, UK.

The authors and publishers are grateful to the following copyright owners for permission to reproduce copyright material. Every endeavour has been made to contact copyright owners and apologies are expressed for any omissions.

Süddeutsche Zeitung and Dr. Rudolph Schütz for the quotations on p. 9 from Süddeutsche Zeitung Magazine no. 21/95; New Scientist for the text on p. 15; Boxtree Ltd. for the extracts from *The Fun and Games Puzzle Book* on pp. 24–25; The Guardian for the article by William Mayes **on** p. 34, © The Guardian; Philippe Roy for the Tarte Flambée material on p. 35; Future Publishing Ltd. for the PC Format cover on p. 43, © 1993 Future Publishing Limited. Used by permission. All rights reserved; Toyota (GB) Limited for the advert on p. 43; Benetton for the advert on p. 47 (B), © Benetton; The National Opinion Research Centre at the University of Chicago for the questionnaire on p. 53; Robert E. Rogoff for *Dessert* by Robert E. Rogoff on p. 55, Copyright © 1995 Robert E. Rogoff. All rights reserved; Die Abendzeitung for the text and content of the egg paintings on pp. 62 & 100; Punch Library for the cartoons on p. 63 (A, C, D & F); Private Eye for the cartoons on p. 63 (B & E); The Times for the article on p. 68 by Bill Frost and Kathryn Knight, the articles on p. 91 by Andrew Malone (tl) and Jon Ashford (tr), the article on p. 101 by Simon Jenkins, and The Sunday Times for the article on p. 91 (b), © Times Newspapers Limited, (1994 and 1995); HarperCollins *Publishers* Limited for the story 'Zoo' by Edward D. Koch taken from *Young Extraterrestrials* on p. 109.

The authors and publishers are grateful to the following illustrators, photographers and photographic sources:

Illustrators: Peter Byatt: pp. 24, 25, 92; Paul Davies: p. 23; Paul Dickinson: p. 31; Max Ellis: p. 55; Hilary Evans: pp. 10, 61; Gecko Limited: all DTP illustrations and graphics; Helena Greene: p. 33; Sue Hillwood-Harris: p. 30; Phil Healey: pp. 9, 46, 71; Amanda MacPhail: pp. 18, 51, 81, 96; Michael Ogden: pp. 11, 97 tr, 97 br; Pantelis Palios: pp. 14, 27, 73, 86; Tracy Rich: pp. 15 b, 58; Martin Sanders: pp. 62, 67, 100; Brian Smith: p. 29; Kath Walker: pp. 13, 69; Colin Wheeler: p. 15 t; Dan Williams: p. 44; Rosemary Woods: p. 78; Annabel Wright: pp. 53, 63 t, 74, 103.

Photographic sources: Ace Photo Agency: p. 12 (9); Allsport/Russell Cheyne: p. 22 (inset); François Gohier/Ardea London: p. 70; Art Directors Photo Library: pp. 64 (B), 65 r, 87 (D); John Gilbert/Aspect Picture Library: p. 49 l; Portrait of Marco Polo (1254–1324), by Dolfino (litho), Biblioteca Nazionale, Turin/Bridgeman Art Library, London: p. 21 r, Portrait of Shakespeare, engraving by Droeshurt, 1623, British Library, London/BAL, London: p. 87 (B), *Self Portrait with Bandaged Ear*, 1889, by Vincent Van Gogh (1853-90), Courtauld Institute Galleries, University of London/BAL London: p. 47 (G), Little Red Riding Hood, by Arthur Rackham (1867–1939), Private Collection/BAL London. 'The Arthur Rackham pictures are reproduced with the kind permission of his family': p. 19 t, *The Sick Child*, 1907, by Edvard Munch (1863–1944), Tate Gallery, London/BAL London, © The Munch Museum/The Munch-Ellingsen Group/DACS 1997: p. 20; British Council Collection: p. 90; Britstock/Eric Bach: p. 38 (D), Britstock/R. Schuhmann: p. 65 bm; Camera Press Limited: pp. 28 t, 49 tr, 87 (G); The J. Allan Cash Photolibrary: p. 101; Chris Coggins: pp. 8, 12 (1, 2, 7 & 8), 33, 35, 42, 45, 62, 64 b, 88, 100; Corbis-Bettmann/UPI: p. 82 tl; Empics/Presse Sports: p. 47 (F); Mary Evans Picture Library: p. 21 l, MEPL/Michael Buhler: p. 38 (B); Chris Fairclough Colour Library: p. 12 (5); David Sillitoe/The Guardian, © The Guardian, p. 34; Robert Harding Picture Library: pp. 40, 49 br, RHPL/Nigel Francis: p. 47 (H); Sarah Murray/Hutchison: p. 47 (A); Images Colour Library: pp. 19 b, 22 (E & F); John Arthur/Impact Photos: p. 83 m, David Reed/Impact: p. 73 b, Simon Shepheard/Impact: p. 12 (4); Kenji Kawakami for the photographs taken from 101 *Unuseless Japanese Inventions*: pp. 59, 87 (F) and 99; 'Popeye' reproduced by kind permission of TM & © 1996 King Features Syndicate Inc.: p. 65 bl; Universal/Kobal: p. 47 (D); David Heyelin/NHPA: p. 73 t, Rod Planck/NHPA: p. 72 (B), Andy Rouse/NHPA: p. 87 (A); 'PA News' Photo Library: p. 28 b; Ron Giling/Panos Pictures: pp. 87 (C), 102 b, Jeremy Hartley/Panos: p. 72 (D); The Photographers Library: pp. 22 (A), 48; Pictor International: pp. 12 (6), 72 (A), 87 (H); Pictures Colour Library: p. 64 (C); Popperfoto: p. 82 mr; Private Collection: p. 89; Raymonds Press Agency, Derby: p. 68; Rex Features Limited: pp. 22 (D), 102 t, Rex Features/The Sun: p. 91; *Regarding Soup* and *Sirens Rising* by Gabriella Roth, © 1994 Gabriella Roth: pp. 39 & 94; Roswell Footage Limited: p. 38 (C); Scott Camazine/Science Photo Library: p. 98; Spindrift Photos/David Pratt: p. 85; Frank Spooner Pictures/Gamma: pp. 47 (C), 64 (D), 82 tr, 82 br; Tony Stone Images/Kevin Kelley: p. 52, TSI/Lester Lefkowitz: p. 38 (A), TSI/David Madison: pp. 22 (B & C), TSI/Joseph McBride: p. 22 t, TSI/Marc Pokemprier: p. 60; Georges De Keerle/Sygma: p. 65 ml, Brooks Kraft/Sygma: p. 87 (E), Richard Melloul/Sygma: p. 83 r, François Poincet/Sygma: p. 80, Mathieu Polak/Sygma: p. 12 (3), P. Le Segretain/Sygma: p. 83 l, Randy Taylor/Sygma: p. 82 bl; Telegraph Colour Library/FGP: p. 93, TCL/Ian Sanderson: p. 72 (C); Viewfinder Colour Photo Library: p. 47 (E).

We have been unable to trace the copyright holders for the pictures on p. 64 (A), taken from 'Tatoo, The Exotic Art of Skin Decoration', by Michelle Delio and p. 65 tl by George Selleck/Bodyworks. We would be grateful for any information that would enable us to do so.

t = top   m = middle   b = bottom   r = right   l = left

Picture research by Sandie Huskinson-Rolfe of PHOTOSEEKERS.
Cover design by Dunne & Scully.
Design and production handled by Gecko Limited, Bicester, Oxon.
Colour scanning and reproduction by Goodfellow & Egan, Cambridge.
Permissions cleared by Sophie Dukan.
Sound recordings by Martin Williamson, Prolingua Productions at Studio AVP.
Freelance editorial work by Meredith Levy.